IMAGES
of America

WASHINGTON
CANOE CLUB

HISTORIC BOATHOUSE. The emblem of the Washington Canoe Club (WCC) is a canoe imposed on a W, encircled. It hangs below the balcony on WCC's wood-shingle boathouse. Built in 1904–1905 and added to over time, the building is a prominent feature on the Georgetown waterfront. It was designated a DC landmark in 1973 and added to the National Register of Historic Places in 1991. (Courtesy of Historic American Building Survey, National Park Service.)

ON THE COVER: WASHINGTON CANOE CLUB. Its landmark Victorian-style boathouse forms the backdrop for a festive day in the 1920s at the Washington Canoe Club. Flags hanging from the balcony and the stylish dress of the men and women suggest a major regatta is on tap. Spectators seem to be poised for an event to begin. While some paddlers prepare for a race, others are out for a leisurely float. (Courtesy of WCC.)

IMAGES
of America

WASHINGTON
CANOE CLUB

Christopher N. Brown

ARCADIA
PUBLISHING

Published by Arcadia Publishing
Charleston, South Carolina

Printed in the United States of America

Library of Congress Control Number: 2019956102

For all general information, please contact Arcadia Publishing:
Telephone 843-853-2070
Fax 843-853-0044
E-mail sales@arcadiapublishing.com
For customer service and orders:
Toll-Free 1-888-313-2665

Visit us on the Internet at www.arcadiapublishing.com

DEDICATION. This book is dedicated to the generations of spirited, fun-loving paddlers who have given life to the Washington Canoe Club and advanced the art of paddling. Among them were club members preparing to welcome home WCC's first Olympians in 1924. (Courtesy of WCC.)

CONTENTS

ACKNOWLEDGMENTS

This book is as much a collaboration as an individual endeavor, and I am indebted to almost 100 people who contributed generously and encouraged me along the way. But there are a number of individuals who deserve to be called out.

I could not have done the book without Bonnie and Dan Havens and Ursula Rhodes opening their homes and family albums to me; I am deeply appreciative. Longtime canoeing pal Sam Stokes provided expert guidance from start to finish as well as many, many hours of rigorous editing. Similarly, Jim Ross was my wingman and inexhaustible source of information, edits, encouragement, and obscure leads. My friends Herb Howe, Baird Smith, Pam Boteler, Cheryl Zook, Debby Page, and Dodge Havens repeatedly gave me invaluable information and critical reviews of drafts. Blaise Rhodes, Ben Sullivan, Dave Winer, Kathy Summers, and Jerry McCoy (of the DC Public Library) were virtual firemen, time and again racing to my rescue with timely photographs and information. Marcus Lundmark, Alexandra and Mike Harbold, Francine Fox, Dorcas Adkins, Pat Munoz, and Andrew Soles contributed very helpful history and comments along the way. An enormous thank you to all.

Special thanks go to Caroline Anderson and Erin Vosgien, my editors at Arcadia Publishing, whose record of near-instantaneous responses to my endless inquiries was both astonishing and a godsend; to Jessica Smith at the Historical Society of Washington for special attention in opening the society's resources to me; and to Gigi Price, whose Historic American Building Survey (National Park Service) report on the canoe club was my essential guide.

My wife, Mary, was my indispensable, daily companion on this project, at once consultant, skilled editor, photographer, tech support, comforter, and advisor of last resort. Without her, there would be no book.

Even with all this help, I am responsible and regret the errors that will inevitably appear. I would be grateful to have them pointed out to me.

Finally, I want to acknowledge the late Ralph Frese, a fourth-generation blacksmith in Chicago, canoe builder, keeper of the voyageur tradition, and raconteur *sans pareil*, who kindled my interest in canoeing 50 years ago. How often can one say someone truly changed your life? Ralph changed mine.

PHOTO CREDITS:

To the many gifted photographers who stepped up to enrich the book: I have recognized you in credit lines but want also to express my thanks for your generosity. Abbreviations used throughout are as follows: DCPL for DC Public Library and WCC for Washington Canoe Club. Learn more about the Washington Canoe Club by visiting its website: www.washingtoncanoeclub.org.

INTRODUCTION

Behind the wood shingle walls of Georgetown's landmark Washington Canoe Club (WCC)lie a bundle of contradictions. Located on the broad Potomac, the boathouse has been an oasis of calm in the busy city while also, over its history, vibrating with paddlers and activity. Intensely competitive on race days, club life has been otherwise sociable and collaborative. Once hewing to prevailing conservative social norms, the club became a home for pioneering women paddlers. And while a private refuge for its members, the WCC has reached out to contribute its share to the civic life of the nation's capital. The canoe club's story encompasses all of these things.

Founded in 1904, the WCC has been a fixture on the Georgetown waterfront for over a century. Its iconic Victorian shingle-style boathouse is a designated Washington, DC, landmark and is listed in the National Register of Historic Places. It is one of only two remaining historic boat clubs of what was once a "boathouse row" on the Potomac River and now lies within the boundaries of the Chesapeake & Ohio National Historical Park. Located in the floodplain of the Potomac, it has narrowly escaped destruction from floods, ice jams, and hurricanes; it has also faced and overcome threats from changing adjacent land uses. The club and boathouse are survivors.

The WCC is the story of a community of athletes. From the outset, competition has been central to the club's raison d'etre, and WCC paddlers have succeeded at the highest levels of their sport. Twenty-eight members have been on Olympic teams, and the club has produced hundreds of national and international champions. Two WCC athletes have reached the pinnacle of amateur athletics glory, winning Olympic gold medals; two others have won silver. These WCCers are four of only nine Americans ever to win Olympic medals in flatwater paddling events.

The WCC is also a family venue that has given generations of adults and kids a respite from the hubbub and hot summers of Washington—a riverfront spot to relax and recharge and a chance to devote abundant energies to racing, building, repairing, and playing. For many members, the canoe club has been the hub of their social lives.

On another level, the canoe club's history demonstrates the evolution of outdoor recreation and social clubs in post–Civil War America, when people began to enjoy newfound leisure in the great outdoors. Americans sought camaraderie and association in their activities, whether bicycling, birding, hiking, or paddling, and various clubs and societies were established to enable and promote their interests. New types of canoes and kayaks were being produced at prices affordable to a growing middle class. Further, at a time of increased concern for health and wellness, a "physical culture" movement emerged, emphasizing training and strengthening to improve body and mind. WCC was committed to "mutual improvement, the promotion of physical culture and the art of canoeing." The club fielded teams in multiple sports in addition to paddling; members regularly competed in everything from football and wrestling to baseball and bowling, with the most athletic of them active in several sports. Looking through early club records, one wonders how WCCers had time to go to work!

The club as a social institution also represents the mores of its times. Never overloaded with luminaries or the socially prominent, the club was described by Dodge Havens as "an eclectic mixture of social classes brought together by a common love of canoeing" and early members (as those today) came from a range of occupations, including business, the professions, the trades, and the civil service. But membership was open only to white males. There was a men's smoking lounge and male-only events; wives and girlfriends were welcome and frequent visitors but played support roles. Change came slowly. Women began competing regularly in paddling events before 1920, and a women's locker room was added to the boathouse. But it was another 50 years before women could be full members of the WCC. And in the segregated life of Washington in the first half of the 20th century, African Americans were infrequent visitors to the club and did not participate in its main events.

At the same time, the WCC has a history of pioneering and innovation that distinguishes it from other DC institutions. WCC men played a prominent role in introducing canoeing as an Olympic event in 1924 and were leaders as rules and standards for international canoes and kayaks advanced. Long before the 1970s brought more equity for women's athletics, women were paddling competitively at the canoe club, and the first American woman to qualify for an Olympic paddling event (in 1952) was from the WCC. Two of the first three Olympic paddling medals won by US women paddlers went to WCCers. The club became the national hub of women's kayaking, and its women have been leaders in the global fight for inclusion and gender equality in paddling.

The WCC has always been engaged with the Greater DC community. From gaining the support of Pres. Calvin Coolidge in 1925 to sponsor the President's Cup Regatta (a combination of on-river competitions that continued as a Washington institution for almost half a century) to hosting wounded warriors and inner-city youth paddlers, the club has been committed to advancing paddle sports and ensuring that many can enjoy being on the water and have the skills to do it safely. For the unprepared, careless, or unlucky, WCC members have acted as first responders to tip-overs and more serious mishaps. Club lore contains many stories of dramatic rescues.

In sum, the WCC has been a place of refreshment and renewal for its members, a host and innovator for paddling, and a contributor in many ways to the life of the city. Even with the enormous societal changes since its founding, the club's new mission stays true to its historic role: "The Washington Canoe Club is a community of volunteers dedicated to preserving, promoting, and engaging in paddlesports on the Potomac River." But the club has new aspirations, too, including restoring its historic clubhouse, encouraging a more diverse group of paddlers at all levels, and serving as a beacon for river safety and enlightened stewardship of the Potomac. While continuing its long traditions of "mutual improvement" and volunteerism, the club seeks to extend its reach over its second century to enrich the lives of its members and the civic life of Greater DC.

One

THE BEGINNINGS

Following the Civil War, America saw major changes in lifestyles and attitudes about leisure and the outdoors. Where nature had often meant challenge and adversity to early settlers, post–Civil War Americans, many more now living in cities, saw the outdoors as a balm: a place to refresh and reenergize. A more concentrated population and increased leisure time for many set the stage for the development of sports and recreation that are now part of American life. Organized sports like football and baseball became national pastimes for both participants and spectators. Rowing and roller-skating gained popularity, and by the 1890s, bicycling was considered a nationwide craze. A growing awareness of the costs to people's health from more sedentary city life also helped create enthusiasm for exercise in the outdoors, and numerous fraternal organizations, from hiking and bicycling groups to birding and boat clubs, grew up around the country.

Canoeing was very much part of this movement. Long the province of Native Americans, explorers, and fur traders, canoes became more popular in the late 19th century as the craft became more affordable and durable. The American Canoe Association was founded in 1880 in response to the widespread interest in paddling and to foster communication among the many local groups around the country that had formed; emphasis was on promoting skills and camaraderie and increasingly on racing. The city of Washington, growing more quickly after the Civil War, had a long history of boat clubs, dating back to about 1840, but most had been focused on rowing. The Potomac Boat Club and the Analostan Club took in canoeists during the 1880s and 1890s but were essentially rowing clubs.

According to contemporaneous press accounts, a group of men came together in 1884 to form a "Washington Canoe Club," but that organization "flickered out after a brief existence," according to the December 6, 1927, *Washington Post*. What is known today as the Washington Canoe Club (WCC) was founded in 1904. Paddlers from other clubs and newcomers to the city were eager to have their own place to socialize and focus on paddle sports (rather than rowing) and to use as a base for canoe races and regattas. They secured a spot 100 yards upriver from the then most prominent landmark on the Potomac, the Aqueduct Bridge, and built themselves a boathouse.

PADDLING. Native Americans had built and used canoes (and in the north, kayaks) for thousands of years before European settlement. Primarily for transportation, birchbark canoes continued in common use well into the 19th century, even as craftsmen began to build all-wood and wood-and-canvas canoes for a broader public. Here, an Indian family (possibly Ojibwe, given the canoe design) travels by canoe. (Courtesy of Library of Congress.)

RECREATION IN THE 19TH CENTURY. In the late 19th century, various organized sports became popular as Americans had more leisure time. Baseball and football were team sports that attracted large numbers of participants and spectators; boxing, horse racing, cockfighting, and yacht racing were also popular. Individuals learned to roller-skate and play golf or enjoy noncompetitive outdoor activities like birdwatching. (Courtesy of Library of Congress.)

BICYCLING POPULARITY. A group poses during a bicycle excursion in Denver, Colorado, in the late 19th century. Bicycling had become a national craze in the 1890s following the invention of the safety bicycle (with equal-sized wheels and pneumatic tires); along with rowing, it was considered "the most fashionable sport" in Washington, according to DC historian James Goode. Bicycle clubs formed all over the country, and a national League of American Wheelmen was founded in 1880. (Courtesy of History Colorado, Charles S. Lillybridge Photographs Collection.)

ATHLETIC AND SOCIAL CLUBS. The shift to city living led, for many Americans, to a more sedentary lifestyle. Reformers advocated "physical culture" programs to improve overall health; their movement promoted specific exercise regimes and sports like fencing, boxing, and wrestling. Athletic clubs, typically all-male and segregated, offered the opportunity for socializing as well as exercise. This early photograph of the WCC's wrestling team includes Olympic paddler Charles "Bud" Havens, standing at left. (Courtesy of Dan and Bonnie Havens.)

ROWING. Rowing, or crew as competitive rowing is known, has ancient roots, and crew competitions were well-established along the Potomac by the 1870s, with races often drawing huge crowds. Rowers utilize oars and face backwards as they propel their craft (sculls or shells) through the water. Pictured at left is Pat Dempsey, Georgetown University's crew coach, heading upriver from Georgetown in a "single" while coaching a pair of "eights" in 1909. (Courtesy of DCPL– Peabody Room.)

PADDLING. Canoeists (and kayakers) use paddles and face forwards in the boat. They may use single or double-blade paddles and paddle alone or with partners. Here, two WCC paddlers (c. 1915) race across the Potomac with the Aqueduct Bridge in the background. (Courtesy of WCC.)

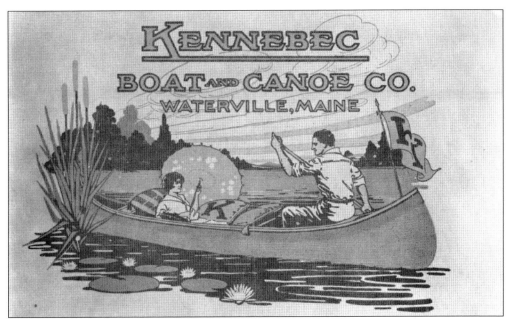

EARLY CANOEING. Canoe manufacturers like the Kennebec Boat and Canoe Company of Waterville, Maine, began making inexpensive wood-and-canvas craft in the late 19th century. A wood frame and hull were covered with canvas and painted to be watertight. Some canoes were specially built with back-facing front seats for couples seeking a pleasant romantic outing free from chaperones. (Courtesy of Wooden Canoe Heritage Association.)

PIONEERS. A few daring women, dressed with appropriate taste and modesty for their adventure, modeled "the benefit of water sports" in solo canoes, rowing shells, and at the helm of motor launches. A 1906 *Washington Times* writer preached: "Where there is water of any sort . . . near you, manage to get plenty of the splendid exercise which handling a boat of any sort is sure to offer occasion for." (Courtesy of DCPL, Washingtoniana Collection.)

CANOEING POPULARITY. According to a 1927 *Washington Post* article, "Canoeing was rather slow in coming into favor as a river sport in Washington and up to 1884 there were only half a dozen men who owned canoes and not above 25 of these craft in the whole city." But this early-1900s postcard of the Potomac River, near Haines Point, shows that the sport had taken off in the city by the turn of the 20th century. (Courtesy of Historical Society of Washington, DC.)

CANOE CLUBS. The Sycamore Island Canoe Club was Washington's first canoe-only club, founded in 1885. Located on the Potomac four miles upriver from the city, the club enjoyed an idyllic setting on an island reachable only by a hand-operated ferry. As more recreational canoes came into use in the late 19th and early 20th centuries, canoe clubs sprang up around the United States and Canada. The Sycamore Island club is still thriving in 2019. (Courtesy of Sycamore Island Canoe Club.)

A Club for "Paddlers of Canoes." This headline in the September 3, 1905, *Washington Post* formally announced the new Washington Canoe Club and its planned boathouse. The club was founded in 1904 to provide its members the opportunity for "mutual improvement [and] the promotion of physical culture and the art of canoeing." All of the club's founding officers had left the Potomac Boat Club, apparently over that club's emphasis on rowing over paddling, and around 1900 had joined the tiny High Island Canoe Club, located on an island upriver near Little Falls. A clubhouse (which later burned) was built on the island in 1901. Soon afterwards, seeking more space as well as calmer waters for paddling, the WCC founders chose the club's current tidewater location at the upper end of Georgetown and launched the WCC. Initial membership was limited to 100. William Fracker was the first president, with Carl Stodder, Lawrence Eberbach, William B. Whipple, W. Ray Garret, and John O. LaGorce the other founding officers. The article described the proposed WCC boathouse as a place for "devotees of idyllic sport" that would be the "best equipped on the Potomac . . . thoroughly heated, and with handsome smoking and ladies' rooms." (Courtesy of WCC.)

15

GEORGETOWN WATERFRONT. At the turn of the 20th century, mills and warehouses dotted the Potomac shoreline below Georgetown University, as seen in this 1889 *Leslie's Weekly* sketch from the Aqueduct Bridge. The WCC's founders saw the potential for a new boathouse there and in 1905 signed a one-year lease (for $100) with the Chesapeake & Ohio Canal Company for a strip of land running 400 feet along the riverbank (between the two large white buildings in the image). (Courtesy of DCPL, WCC Collection.)

EARLY CLUB MEMBERS. From left to right, Jim Burch, Reginald Rutherford, Bill Rogers, and Hans Wagner pose around 1920 with their double-blade paddles. All were distinguished racers. Rogers came to DC from Nova Scotia, where he had competed in Canadian Canoe Association meets. He became the WCC's coach and commodore and is credited with much of the club's early paddling success, introducing both war canoes (for conditioning) and single-blade paddling techniques. Rogers later took leadership roles in the President's Cup Regatta. (Courtesy of WCC.)

Two

A Home for the Club

From the outset, the WCC's founders had their hearts set on building a handsome, well-appointed boathouse. Riverbank land was quickly secured by lease with the Chesapeake & Ohio Canal Company in 1905 and construction commenced. While boat launch and storage were its principal functions, the boathouse, with its narrow porch and later a concrete apron out front, its riverside balconies, and its ample interior spaces, has been the home for the club's myriad competitive and social events ever since.

The building was designed by an early club member, architect George Percival Hales, a recent arrival in town who was familiar with boathouse design from his time paddling on the Charles River in Boston. The WCC structure is an excellent example of Victorian shingle-style architecture made popular in the late 19th century. Its facade, with a pronounced cross-gable anchored by octagonal turrets, make it a DC waterfront icon. Inside, in addition to boat racks and locker rooms, the boathouse has social spaces, including a generous second-floor ballroom with fireplace and stage—the venue for a century of dances, masquerades, banquets, theatricals, and other club traditions. The boathouse is one of only two historic boat clubs still standing on the Georgetown waterfront; it is a designated DC landmark and is listed in the National Register of Historic Places.

The boathouse was built in three stages as funds became available and needs expanded. Club lore has it that the initial construction was accomplished by charter members using mostly salvaged lumber. The building was constructed on piers over the Potomac River, with pedestrian access from the rear to the second floor by catwalk from the Chesapeake and Ohio (C&O) Canal towpath. While largely completed by 1922, the boathouse has continued to be modified and upgraded over the years.

Congress established the Chesapeake & Ohio Canal National Historical Park in 1971. With the boathouse now within park boundaries, the National Park Service (NPS) came to have an increased management involvement. In 2010, concerned that deterioration made the building unsafe for occupancy, the NPS closed it to club use and undertook temporary stabilization measures. It also documented the structure in its Historic American Building Survey. In 2019, the WCC's home was in dilapidated condition, awaiting restoration, but its essential and beloved architectural character still graced the Potomac shore.

VICTORIAN INSPIRATION FOR WCC. Architect George P. Hales (1880–1970), recently arrived in Washington from Massachusetts, brought his experience paddling on the Charles River near Boston (above) to the WCC design. The Victorian elements of New England boathouses and summer cottages—wood shingles, hipped roofs, gables, and capacious porches and balconies—would be incorporated in the WCC boathouse to achieve a blend of rusticity with comfort. (Courtesy of Library of Congress.)

DRAMATIC TOWERS. To lend elegance and romance to the planned WCC boathouse, architect Hales included a tower in his design like that of the nearby Potomac Boat Club (PBC), pictured here hosting an overflow regatta crowd in 1904. The PBC's grand boathouse (replaced in 1908 by its current home) was built in the 1870s in the middle of Georgetown's commercial waterfront. The tall wooden trestle on the right had rails for hand carts that were used to transit coal and other bulk materials from C&O Canal barges to the Potomac docks and waiting ships. (Courtesy of DCPL–Peabody Room.)

WCC's First Home. The WCC boathouse, nearing the end of its initial construction (c. 1905), generally follows the architect's published sketch (see page 15), with tower, decorative fan window, and cupola. Doors have been added to allow easier access to boats. The wooden pilings of 10-inch-by-10-inch southern yellow pine, visible here, supported the structure above the Potomac, with only the north side of the building anchored to the shore. In the background are the spires of Georgetown University's Healy Hall. (Courtesy of WCC.)

Do-It-Yourself. Club members, here working on the west turret, built the new boathouse using in part salvaged lumber. The work was financed with a $1,000 prize from a *Washington Post* subscription contest and proceeds from a benefit dance and a minstrel show (a then-popular entertainment that became unacceptable and clearly offensive in later years). The initial building permit lists R.Z. Hazell & Brothers as the builder of record, but founding club members Cleve Skinker and Ray Garret, who owned a construction company, likely played a support role in erecting the structure. The volunteer tradition of repair and upkeep of the boathouse remains strong in 2019. (Courtesy of WCC.)

PHASE 1, 1905–1906. The completed WCC boathouse included boat storage on the ground floor, a ballroom and men's locker room on the second, and a full ramp running down to the docks. Generous balconies overlooked the river, and a fireplace and oil stoves provided heat. The truncated appearance suggests the intention was always to include a second tower. (Courtesy of the William "Dusty" Rhodes family.)

PHASE 2, 1910. "Canoeists' Home Doubled in Size" touted a 1910 headline in the *Washington Times*. A loan financed the addition of a second turret and small side porch, making the building symmetrical and more picturesque. There was now space for the planned smoking room, grill room, and kitchen on the first floor and a meeting room and ladies' dressing room on the second. Note that the tops of towers are open-air. (Courtesy of WCC.)

PHASE 3, C. 1922. With expanding membership and women paddling competitively, the club added a downriver section (on the right) with a women's locker room upstairs and three boat storage bays below. In 1932, members repainted the club green (from the original red). With white paint outlining the doors and windows, the boathouse was described in the nomination for the National Register of Historic Places as "a sculptural element in the riverside landscape." The 15-man Peterborough war canoe in the foreground was popular for racing in the first half of the 20th century. (Courtesy of Dan and Bonnie Havens.)

SUBJECT FOR ARTISTS. As the only wood-shingle Victorian-style boathouse on the entire DC waterfront, the canoe club is an icon and has attracted many painters, including local artist Allen Cross, who did this watercolor in 1996. The low roof added on the east end in the mid-1970s provided indoor workshop space for boat repair; a wide stairway (far right) gave access to the second-floor workspace. In addition to painters and photographers, the charming setting has served as a backdrop in films, including the 1990s thriller *Enemy of the State*. (Courtesy of Sheldon and Mary Beth Ray.)

NARROW PORCH. Prior to 1970 and the construction of a large-scale underground sewer project in front of the boathouse, there was only a five-foot-wide wooden deck on the river side of the boathouse, with large ramps leading down to the docks. The unidentified woman in the photograph is ready for a swim or simply to relax in the rocking chairs. In the distance, one can see Dempsey's Boathouse jutting out below the Key Bridge. (Courtesy of the William "Dusty" Rhodes family.)

TOWERS. The most striking features of the WCC boathouse are its two imposing turrets, captured here in an oil painting by Gonzalo Ruiz Navarro. Each has a small octagonal room near the top where, over the decades, young, impecunious WCC members and visiting athletes (and even couples) have lived for extended periods. In exchange for custodial services, these residents enjoyed free lodging (albeit with limited amenities, for example no heat) at a highly desirable riverside address. (Courtesy of Gonzalo Ruiz Navarro.)

BALLROOM, C. 1909. Central to club social functions has been the impressive second-floor ballroom, with its vaulted ceiling, horizontal planking of the walls, and windows looking out on three sides. The view from the east windows (on the right) was cut off with the 1910 addition. The ballroom has had a succession of hanging canoes to celebrate its heritage; this one is birchbark. Over time, trophy cases (filled with dozens of silver trophies), columns to support the ceiling, and built-in benches were added. The original corbelled fireplace welcomed members, making the room a warm place to congregate, have a smoke, and swap yarns (below). Opposite the fireplace was a bandstand (not pictured). The WCC became a second home to many members and their families. (Both, courtesy of the William "Dusty" Rhodes family.)

23

FOUNDING CLUB MEMBERS. A colorful 26-panel cartoon mural runs 67 feet around the first-floor Grill Room in the boathouse. The frieze (24–27 inches high) depicts in caricature many of the 100 charter members of the club in amusing and uncomplimentary poses: paddling, play-acting, carousing, and swilling beer out of large mugs. From the outset, WCCers have come from a cross-

CLUB FUN. The sheet music on the piano (in this detail from the mural) is titled "Roosevelt in Africa," believed to be a musical number from a club theatrical lampooning the former president's safari to Africa in 1909. Roosevelt and his party bagged 512 large animals on the trip and collected over 11,000 specimens for the Smithsonian Institution. (Courtesy of John Burwell.)

section of professions and trades; the club has had few nationally prominent members in its ranks, except, of course, its paddling champions. For some, the mural is an uncomfortable reminder of an era when all-male, all-white social clubs were common; it can be jarring to 21st-century sensibilities. (Courtesy of John Burwell.)

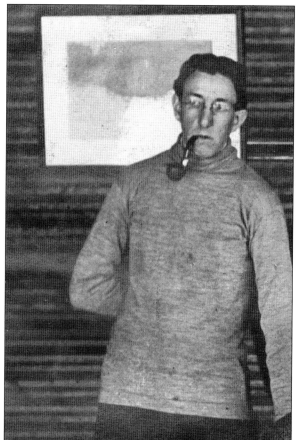 

THE ARTIST. Felix Mahoney (1867–1939), an early WCC member, painted the mural around 1910. He was an award-winning cartoonist for the *Washington Evening Star* and the founder and director of the National School of Fine and Applied Arts in Washington. At the WCC, in addition to paddling, he sang in numerous theatricals and also in local operas. The mural includes a self-portrait of Mahoney, above right. (Left, courtesy of WCC; right, courtesy of John Burwell.)

A PLACE IN LEGOLAND. What could be a higher validation for the architectural significance of the WCC than to be included, along with the White House, US Capitol, and other signature Washington buildings, in Miniland USA at California's Legoland? The Lego artisan faithfully captures the original siting of the boathouse on piers over the river and its narrow porch but takes a few liberties with the building itself as well as with the setting. (Courtesy of WCC.)

LOGO AND TOTEM. While the encircled canoe imposed on a W is the official emblem of the WCC, the owl is the club totem. Legend has it that, as the founding WCC members sat resting from a hard day installing the ridge pole of the boathouse, an owl flew in and perched above them in the open rafters. It was taken as a good omen, and the owl (here a stylized wood cutout) has benevolently watched over the club and its endeavors ever since. (Courtesy of the author.)

Three

LIFE AND HARD TIMES ALONG THE POTOMAC

The Washington Canoe Club has been very much part of a riverside community—of competitors, of buildings, of "river rats"—since its founding in 1904. It is a rich history.

Far from being an isolated, stand-alone structure, the boathouse during its 115-year span has been in the midst of various configurations of mills, warehouses, sheds, docks, railroad outbuildings, icehouses, shacks, camps, and other buildings. In fact, every historic photograph of the WCC up until the 1960s shows a different array of neighboring structures.

The WCC boathouse was hardly the first in Washington. Beginning in the 1840s, there were clubhouses on the old City Canal (which ran along what is now Constitution Avenue), and on the tidal Potomac, there were at least five early boathouses. They were mostly rowing clubs or facilities that rented canoes and other boats.

Predating the WCC, too, was the tradition of camping out on the Potomac. Long before residential air-conditioning was common, the river provided relief from the summer heat. Literally dozens of encampments grew up along both shores of the Potomac between the Key and Chain Bridges and even farther up to Great Falls. WCC historian William "Dusty" Rhodes rhapsodized that "in those golden years . . . the beautiful Potomac brought surcease to the tired and jaded citizens who made evening and weekly pilgrimages to its cool and inspiring shores." At the camps there was a flourishing social life as well as frequent competitions that honed the racing skills of early WCC athletes.

Being located on the Potomac had its challenges for all these facilities, including the WCC. Storms and fires took their toll on the camps and permanent structures, as did floods. After 1940, water pollution was an issue. Construction of bridges, railroads, and sewer lines and intense squabbles over land use created disruptions and uncertainty. But the designation of the C&O Canal as a national park unit in 1971 protected the land around the WCC on the DC side, so building sites upriver of the Key Bridge were essentially no longer available. Ironically, this gave the WCC a degree of privacy it had never experienced in its previous 70 years.

FUTURE WCC SITE. The Georgetown shoreline in the icy winter of 1889, photographed from the Aqueduct Bridge, shows a prominent feed mill and another structure upstream, with a railroad trestle running along the riverbank. The mill has been identified as that of Tenney & Sons, established in 1870, which produced flour and corn meal utilizing the C&O Canal for waterpower. (Courtesy of WCC.)

EARLIEST WCC BOATHOUSE IMAGE, 1906. The newly constructed Washington Canoe Club, with a single turret, appears to the left of the mill and is seemingly inset in the railroad trestle. Upriver are additional buildings to the right and left of the sailing ship. Farthest in the distance is possibly the remains of the Foxall Foundry, built at the mouth of Foundry Branch. The foundry, also known as the Columbian Foundry, made armaments for the federal government in

RIVERSIDE ACTIVITY. In this pre–WCC photograph (c. 1900), two unidentified workers pose in front of a cabin, with the Tenney mill just upstream and a railroad trestle along the shore. The logs in front of them may be timbers destined for the railroad line; a utility pole and stockade fence are visible in the background, and additional large structures are visible farther upstream. None of these buildings has survived. (Courtesy of Historical Society of Washington, DC.)

the first half of the 19th century, and Henry Foxall has been called "Washington's first defense contractor." The towers of Georgetown University's Healy Hall (constructed 1877–1879) stand atop the ridge, along with Old North (one of the original university buildings) and more recent additions. (Courtesy of WCC.)

WCC and Two Rail Lines. A close examination of this 1905–1906 WCC boathouse photograph shows the railroad trestle with a section removed and the boathouse sitting in the middle. The trestle was, in fact, part of a never-completed rail connection into Georgetown. In the early 1890s, the chartered Washington & Western Maryland Railroad Company planned to connect the thriving Georgetown port to existing rail lines in Maryland and began building; 1892 was the scheduled completion date. It is not clear whether the railroad company or the eager merchants of Georgetown actually undertook the construction, but 4,400 feet of trestle were built along and over the river, and another two miles were laid on land. However, the project was abandoned, the trestle fell into decay, and it was torn down in 1907. The image below captures the brief period (c. 1908) with the mill still in place, the trestle gone, and the 1910 addition to the WCC not yet started. (Above, courtesy of the William "Dusty" Rhodes family; below, courtesy of Historical Society of Washington, DC.)

GEORGETOWN FROM RIVER, WASH., D.C.—#439.

THE SECOND RAIL LINE. In 1906, the Baltimore & Ohio Railroad had proposed a new line, the Georgetown Spur, running along the Potomac shore but behind the WCC to make the connection between Silver Spring and Georgetown. Building of the Georgetown Spur began in 1908, and it was completed in 1910, realizing the long-held dream of Georgetown businesses. After 75 years of carrying building materials, coal, and other freight to the Georgetown waterfront, the spur was abandoned in 1985 after Georgetown was no longer an industrial center. The right-of-way was subsequently converted to the Capital Crescent Trail. The presence of an active rail line right behind boathouse allowed both delivery of supplies and (club lore has it) the convenient loading of canoes for transport to far-away regattas. Members had to travel to these meets separately, however, as the Georgetown Spur was never a passenger route. The short train pictured above (only a steam locomotive, two cars, and a caboose) is a work train backing down the newly laid tracks to support final construction of the road into Georgetown. (Courtesy of DCPL–Peabody Room.)

GATEWAY TO WCC. The archway (above) of the old Aqueduct Bridge (see page 38) has been one entranceway to the WCC for almost its entire 115 years. The arch, originally to support the bridge, became the proposed passageway for a rail line around 1890. But it was too low to accommodate locomotives and train cars, and the height was raised during 1909–1910 construction of the Georgetown Spur rail line. It was a massive engineering undertaking given the active roadway and trolley line still running above. The reconstructed archway (below), with a firm railbed replacing what had been shallow water, gave WCC members a more direct land route to the Georgetown waterfront and streetcar transportation. (Both, courtesy of Library of Congress.)

SUMMER CAMPS. Beginning in the late 19th century and up to the Second World War, Washingtonians would flock to the Potomac River to escape the summer heat. Some would take up long-term residence—a few even living there year-round—setting up camps or building bathhouses, huts, or shanties. A summer community bloomed. Access on the Virginia shore above the Key Bridge was via boat or a gravel road down Spout Run, as there was yet no George Washington Memorial Parkway. To go to work, men of the family would paddle down the river, park their canoes at the WCC or Dempsey's Boathouse, catch streetcars to their jobs, and then return "home" in the evening. In addition to canoeing and swimming, horseshoes and cards were popular. Curiously, ownership of land where all these seasonal squatters set up their encampments is not mentioned in any news accounts. (Both, courtesy of WCC.)

"CAMP STARVATION." The sign on the tree in this 1914 picture tells one of the colorful names for the riverside camps; Hobo Camp, Camp Tut, Camp Goodwill, and Bachelor Camp were others. The Davis Barge, on the Virginia shore upstream of the Key Bridge, was the place to buy soda pop and beer by the bucket during Prohibition; Warner's Canoe House, on the DC side, reportedly had the first jukebox on the river and held Saturday night dances on the dock. (Courtesy of Historical Society of Washington, DC.)

COMPETITION IN THE 1920S. Swimmers start a race from the new WCC docks. With so many vigorous young men and women gathered in camps along the Potomac during the summer, fierce competitions (in addition to picnics and general fun) were frequent. Canoe racing took place on weekends, and WCC old-timers claimed that the intensity of summer-long competition is what led to the club's early racing prowess. (Courtesy of WCC.)

COLONIAL CAMP CANOE CLUB. The two campers at right (c. 1922) are likely from the Colonial Camp, given the insignia on the man's jersey. Colonial was the most elaborate of all the summer establishments. Located on the Virginia shore above the Key Bridge, the camp was laid out in orderly rows, with 16 tents on platforms, providing for sleeping and dining. The mess tent had a dance floor and a Victrola to provide the music. The Colonials had their own successful canoe racing team, which later migrated to the Potomac Boat Club, and their float (similar to the one below) boasted a high dive. Since WCC members could not live in the WCC boathouse, some were also members of Colonial so they could sleep and eat there. After World War II, the park authority no longer allowed camping along the river, and most of the clubs that dotted the Potomac shore were disbanded. (Both, courtesy of Historical Society of Washington, DC.)

SKATING ON THE POTOMAC. Ice skating on the solidly frozen river was a popular wintertime activity for WCC members and many others. However, spring break-up could cause catastrophic conditions, and flooding had been an issue in Washington since its founding. Memorable crests were recorded in 1877, 1889, and 1896, all before the WCC boathouse was constructed. The WCC's time would come. (Courtesy of Dan and Bonnie Havens.)

ICE JAM. On Valentine's Day in 1918, a major thaw caused an ice dam to form at the Fourteenth Street Bridge, which backed up the ice all the way to the Chain Bridge. The dam caused the water to rise 16 feet above normal in Georgetown, threatening the WCC boathouse with huge shards of ice. The WCC sustained $25,000 in damage but survived . . . the first of many remarkable narrow escapes in its history. (Courtesy of Dan and Bonnie Havens.)

BOATHOUSE ROW UNDER ASSAULT. The 1918 ice dam wreaked havoc on the Georgetown waterfront. The WCC's downstream neighbor, Dempsey's Boathouse (on right and at center) had at this time a long boat shed with two-story structures anchoring both ends; the upstream building had a striped roof. Built next to the Aqueduct Bridge in 1903 by Georgetown University rowing coach Patrick Dempsey, the boathouse was expanded 200 feet upriver in the 1910s to accommodate as many as 1,000 canoes. The roof of Dempsey's canoe shed is seen buckling from the crushing pressure of the ice, and the balcony on its boathouse (lower right) hangs perilously over the carnage. Dempsey's entire sprawling establishment was a loss, but after reconstruction, it continued to be a vital canoeing center for another 40 years. Dempsey's was not the only casualty. The pilings of the Analostan Club (located near today's Kennedy Center) were smashed, leaving the boathouse to float away or collapse into the water. The WCC (on the left) had massive ice blocks stacked almost to the second floor but pulled through with limited damage. (Courtesy of Library of Congress.)

ALEXANDRIA AQUEDUCT BRIDGE. Looking northwest (upriver) from today's Roosevelt Island, beyond the Union soldiers in the 1861 photograph above, is the Aqueduct Bridge. With the completion of the C&O Canal in 1833, Georgetown moved into a position to replace Alexandria as the primary port for the nation's capital. Alexandria merchants responded by constructing a canal spur between 1833 and 1843 off the C&O Canal to carry some of that boat traffic across the Potomac and down a canal on the Virginia shore the seven miles to Alexandria. Note the ferry barge (above) crossing the river, carrying horse-drawn buggies toward Georgetown. A canal boat (below) leaves the C&O Canal on the DC shore, heading toward Virginia to begin its journey to Alexandria. The Aqueduct Bridge is a consistent background feature in numerous paddling photographs. (Above, courtesy of Library of Congress; below, courtesy of Historical Society of Washington, DC.)

BRIDGE MODIFICATIONS. Barge traffic across the Aqueduct Bridge was discontinued at the time of the Civil War, and the structure went through major changes over the next 50 years. A second level was added for wagon traffic, followed by removal of the canal trough and repeated rebuildings of the bridge, ending with a steel truss superstructure (pictured) that could support automobiles and trolley tracks. Streetcar service across the span began in 1906, giving WCC members another option to reach the club. (Courtesy of US Army Corps of Engineers, Office of History.)

DOWNSTREAM NEIGHBOR. Only the WCC and Potomac Boat Club (PBC, above in 1925) remain of seven historic Georgetown boathouses. Founded in 1869, the PBC built this, its third and current boathouse, just downstream from the Aqueduct Bridge in 1908. The WCC and PBC have a long, shared history, starting with former PBC members helping found the WCC and continuing with intense paddling rivalries and many joint memberships. A number of PBC paddlers (as well as rowers) were US Olympians, but after about 1970, the PBC became primarily a rowing club. (Courtesy of Library of Congress.)

...getown Bridge.
...o. 98. 9-2-22

40

A Decade of Two Bridges.
Looking toward DC, the Francis
Scott Key Bridge (on the right,
under construction around 1922)
veers downstream of the old
Aqueduct Bridge (left), which then
had trolley tracks and a roadway.
On the far left of the waterfront
is the WCC. Downriver (just to
the left of the Aqueduct Bridge) is
the rebuilt Dempsey's Boathouse:
a double, two-story building with
a long boat shed and ramps to the
water and a single-story building
abutting the WCC at its upriver end.
The Potomac Boat Club is nestled
to the right of the Aqueduct Bridge.
The Key Bridge, authorized in 1916
to replace the aging Aqueduct
Bridge, was constructed from
1920 to 1923, and its huge arches
immediately made it a Washington
landmark; every canoeist has
enjoyed the majesty of paddling
under its vaults. The Aqueduct
Bridge was dismantled in 1933 and
most of its piers removed from the
river in 1962; only a double-arch
abutment on the DC shore and pier
near Virginia remain. (Courtesy
of DCPL, WCC Collection.)

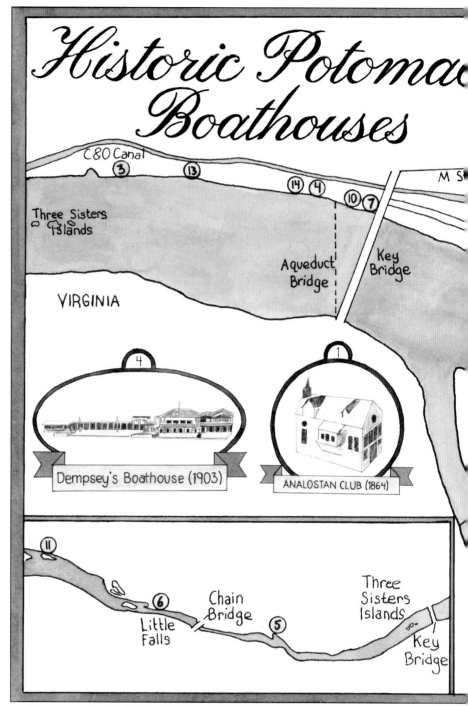

Historic Potoma Boathouses

C&O Canal ③ ⑬ ⑭ ④ ⑩ ⑦ M S

Three Sisters Islands

Aqueduct Bridge

Key Bridge

VIRGINIA

④ Dempsey's Boathouse (1903)

① ANALOSTAN CLUB (1864)

⑪

⑥ Little Falls

Chain Bridge

⑤

Three Sisters Islands

Key Bridge

HISTORY ON THE SHORELINE. Many boathouses have graced the waterways of Washington over the years, some grand edifices, some little more than huts. A few housed rental boats; others were headquarters for clubs. In addition, there were clubs or teams without their own building and also the more ephemeral summer camps of paddlers. Some boathouses were specifically for rowing, others were paddle-oriented, and a few included both rowing and paddle sports. Placement of boathouses

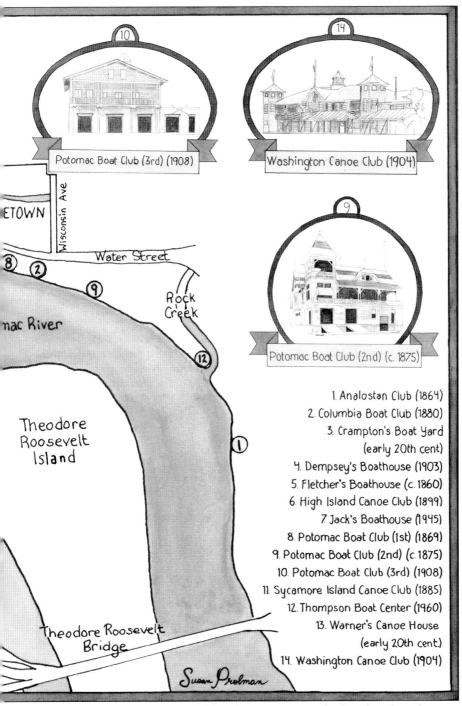

Potomac Boat Club (3rd) (1908)

Washington Canoe Club (1904)

Potomac Boat Club (2nd) (c. 1875)

ETOWN

Wisconsin Ave

Water Street

Rock Creek

mac River

Theodore Roosevelt Island

Theodore Roosevelt Bridge

Susan Prolman

1. Analostan Club (1864)
2. Columbia Boat Club (1880)
3. Crampton's Boat Yard (early 20th cent)
4. Dempsey's Boathouse (1903)
5. Fletcher's Boathouse (c. 1860)
6. High Island Canoe Club (1899)
7. Jack's Boathouse (1945)
8. Potomac Boat Club (1st) (1869)
9. Potomac Boat Club (2nd) (c. 1875)
10. Potomac Boat Club (3rd) (1908)
11. Sycamore Island Canoe Club (1885)
12. Thompson Boat Center (1960)
13. Warner's Canoe House (early 20th cent.)
14. Washington Canoe Club (1904)

on the map is based on best available information, as are the founding dates (in parentheses). Space does not allow depiction of all the boathouses located on the Potomac or those on the historic Washington City Canal, Anacostia River, Washington Channel, or Alexandria waterfront. (Courtesy of Susan Prolman.)

A New Look, c. 1925. The WCC boathouse stands proudly between a row of elegant sheds upstream (which appear to be part of WCC but for which there is no record) and a new two-story structure anchoring Dempsey's boat sheds downstream. This may be the closest the Potomac ever came to matching the grandeur of Philadelphia's famed Schuylkill River Boathouse Row. (Courtesy of WCC.)

Mother Nature. Major floods have been regular events throughout the WCC's history, but the flood of March 1936, following heavy rains and rapid snowmelt, broke all records up to that time. The Potomac watershed, unlike many rivers on the Eastern Seaboard, has no flood control dams on its main stem; this free-flowing river can rampage under the right weather conditions. Here, the water surges around the WCC boathouse near the flood peak. (Courtesy of the William "Dusty" Rhodes family.)

MAJOR FLOODS. Two men ride out the inundation of lower Georgetown early in the 20th century. Sources differ, but either the 1936, 1942, or 1972 flood is considered "the flood of record" at the WCC's location. Other major floods occurred with some regularity, though, including in 1924, 1937, 1948, 1952, 1955, 1985, and most recently in 1996. Several of these events rose above the second floor of the WCC boathouse. (Courtesy of Library of Congress.)

DESTRUCTION. The Potomac floods have been devastating for structures in the floodplain. This boathouse, upstream of the WCC, is possibly Warner's Canoe House, destroyed in the 1936 flood. Again, and again, the WCC boathouse has survived. The good fortune is due in part to a topographic feature: a shoreline indentation that creates an eddy, protecting the club from the river's main current. Boxcars on the Georgetown Spur are visible in the background at left. (Courtesy of WCC.)

EMERGENCY STORAGE, 1930s. WCC members routinely have moved canoes from the boathouse and onto the embankment of the C&O Canal (right) during floods. But it is difficult to predict flood heights and secure all boats; here, several canoes are left floating with logs and other debris. The locomotive in the background, blowing steam, is apparently trying to find a path through the shallow water and clutter to reach Georgetown. (Courtesy of WCC.)

A SAFE PERCH. Once canoes were safely moved to the canal bank, the catwalk bridge connecting the WCC to the C&O Canal towpath provided an ideal viewing spot during the 1936 flood. The catwalk, built around 1910, crossed above the railroad tracks and was the main route to the club's second-floor front door for its first 60 years; it was removed around 1970. (Courtesy of the William "Dusty" Rhodes family.)

FLOOD AFTERMATH. WCC members survey the damage even before the waters have fully receded. Typically, a lot of debris floats in from upstream and collects in front of the WCC, sometimes including useful items such as picnic tables. Some of the canoes, including *Goo Goo* in the foreground, were not pulled to safety ahead of time and so took a hit. The empty whiskey barrels were part of the flotation system for the docks. Inside the boathouse (below), the post-and-beam construction allowed the floodwaters to course through the emptied boat racks during flooding. After the flood ended, a high-pressure hose was used to wash away the mud (pictured here in the 1930s). The original boathouse floor was planking—more like a deck than solid floor—making the clean-up easier. (Both, courtesy of the William "Dusty" Rhodes family.)

DEMISE OF DEMPSEY'S. Dempsey's Boathouse, dating to the year before the WCC's founding (1904) and which had rented canoes to untold thousands, succumbed to a catastrophic fire in 1961. It had fallen into disrepair in the 1950s and was unoccupied and derelict by the end of the decade; the opening of Thompsons Boat Center in 1960, which provided boat rentals and storage at a modern facility, was the final straw. It was a sad end, however, for Dempsey's had been a good neighbor to the WCC and had fielded fine racing teams over the years. The fire, which consumed Dempsey's, was fought from land and water and fortunately did not spread upstream to the nearby WCC nor to the Potomac Boat Club (to the right of the old Aqueduct Bridge abutment). But the blaze provided a very anxious moment for one WCC member who saw "an ominous red glow in the sky" as he drove along Canal Road and assumed the worst; he was relieved to find that the WCC had been spared. (Courtesy of DCPL–Peabody Room.)

Four

COMPETITION AND CRAFT FROM 1900 TO 1959

Competition has been a hallmark of the Washington Canoe Club since its earliest years. While rowing (crew) was well-established on the Potomac River by the end of the 19th century, only three of the early boat clubs also hosted canoeing. The WCC's focus on competitive paddling was new on the Potomac and changed the sport.

The WCC was founded in 1904 as a male-only club. At the beginning, women participated in traditional roles, paddling recreational canoes (often as pampered passengers), cheering on the men in competitions, and participating in dinners and dances. The original clubhouse included a lounge for the ladies, complete with an electric fan. The 1910s and 1920s saw the WCC emerge as the preeminent canoe racing club in the country, and women came into their own as competitive paddlers. The club regularly hosted regattas, frequently coming away with the high-point trophy. To support its female athletes, the 1920 addition to the boathouse included a women's locker room.

With strong advocacy from the WCC and other North American groups, canoe/kayak events were introduced as a demonstration sport in the 1924 Paris Olympic Games by a US/Canadian team. WCC men filled all the US spots and won six medals. Paddling became an official Olympic sport in 1936, and the WCC placed 28 men and women on the US Olympic canoe/kayak teams continuously (in the years the games were held) from 1940 through 1996, more than any other club.

Women's kayak events were added to the Canoeing National Championships in 1938 and to the Olympics in 1948. In 1952, a WCC woman became the first female kayaker to qualify for the US Olympic team, but arcane rules applied by the sport's governing body were used to deny her the opportunity to participate. Finally, in the 1960 Rome Olympics, the United States for the first time officially entered a woman kayaker—again from the WCC—for the sole women's event. WCC men eagerly resumed paddling after their World War II service, winning national championships in several events and placing two paddlers each on the 1948 and 1952 Olympic teams.

The WCC takes pride in having been a major force for introducing canoe/kayak as an Olympic event and, early on, taking steps to provide opportunity and access for women paddlers.

WCC Boating Party. This elegant group, setting out from the WCC dock in the early 20th century, appears to be more concerned with the social opportunities of the outing than with competition, or even with the question of how they will propel themselves, as only a couple of the occupants appear to have paddles. Their very large canoe is from the Old Town Canoe Company. (Courtesy of WCC.)

Spectators. Around 1900, canoeists often watched from the sidelines as rowing crews raced on the Potomac. The Analostan, Columbia, and Potomac boat clubs were the "Big Three" of rowing and drew large crowds for their races but gave less support to paddling. The Aqueduct Bridge provided a good viewing stand for spectators. Note the horse-drawn buggy silhouetted on the bridge. The Potomac River at Washington, while tidal, is usually slow-moving, providing an ideal venue for flatwater racing. (Courtesy of WCC.)

COMPETITION. Canoe racing has defined the WCC since its founding, and having an organization focused on paddling was the major reason that the WCC's founders broke away from other clubs. The WCC's commodore in 1911, W.A. Rogers, recalled: "It was during the summer of 1909 that I first had charge of racing of the Club and it was really the first time that the boys considered the subject seriously enough to get themselves in the proper condition. We worked hard for the [fall] *Washington Post* Regatta . . . and were fortunate enough to win four out of six events consisting of 27 medals and five cups. This aroused the racing spirit enough so that everybody looked forward . . . to the coming season." One of the winning trophies is shown above. Below, paddlers start an Olympic-style four-man canoe race off Haines Point in Washington. (Above, courtesy of the author; below, courtesy of WCC.)

THE PEANUT. This all-purpose boat was the WCC's racing craft of choice for half a century. It could be paddled with either single-blade in the Olympic high-kneel position (left) or double-blade seated (below) with one, two, or four paddlers (the four-person version was a bit larger). Unlike the popular wood-and-canvas canoes of the early 1900s, the peanut was an all-wood, plank-on-frame, flat-profiled craft built in Canada. By the mid-20th century, innovative boat designs and new materials made for much lighter, faster craft, and the peanut became obsolete; it was gradually phased out of racing in the 1950s. At left, the WCC's Everett Rodman, the 1934–1935 National Senior C-1 champion, demonstrates technique. Below, two young paddlers await a double-blade event at the national championships held at the 1939 New York World's Fair. (Left, courtesy of Dan and Bonnie Havens; below, courtesy of Jim Ross.)

WATCHING RACES (PRE-1920). Crowds gather upriver from the WCC to cheer on their favorite teams at a regatta. Newspaper accounts frequently put crowd sizes for boat races in the thousands. The variety of spectator boats—skiffs, canoes, rowboats, a larger pleasure craft with viewers perched atop the cabin, and possibly an electric launch in the background—is matched by the display of stylish hats—ladies in bonnets and mushrooms and men in derbies, bowlers, boaters, and newsboys. As the southernmost of the major canoe clubs on the East Coast, the WCC had a distinct competitive advantage with a longer season for training and racing; athletes from around the country came to the WCC to train. (Courtesy of the William "Dusty" Rhodes family.)

W·C·C· MIXED TANDEM
·1918· 1919· 1920· 1921·
H·T· Knight ~ Miss Elizabeth Smith

WOMEN IN COMPETITION. By 1918, WCC women were no longer being treated as "the weaker sex." Hardly demure in appearance, Elizabeth Smith (paired here with legendary WCC paddler and future Olympian Harry Knight Jr.) is in uniform and looks fully prepared for a race, Olympic (high-kneel) style. Some described her shorts and tunic as "scandalous." The July 31, 1921, *Washington Sunday Star* reported: "Girl canoeists performed well in the regatta. Five couples competed in the mixed doubles that went to Elizabeth Smith, champion girl diver of the District, and Harry Knight of the Washington Canoe Club after a grueling race with Mr. and Mrs. C.B. Eaton, Colonial Canoeists. Mrs. William Havens and Jim Burch of Washington [WCC] finished third. The race was decided over an eighth-mile course." Mixed tandem races were common, and married women were usually referred to under their husband's names. The background scene may be Washington's Haines Point. (Courtesy of WCC.)

REGATTA DAY, 1920. Winners of various events at the 1920 WCC Regatta pose with their haul of silver plates, cups, and trophies. Elizabeth Smith, standing next to Harry Knight Jr. (above, first row, left), is the only woman. Spectators are sitting above the contestants on a barge (seen below) hauled in for the event. Over the club's century-plus, WCC paddlers have won over a thousand junior and senior national and international championships in more than a dozen disciplines while racing throughout North America and in Hawaii, Europe, and southeast Asia. (Above, courtesy of Dan and Bonnie Havens; below, courtesy of WCC.)

AMERICA'S FIRST OLYMPIC CANOEISTS, 1924. From left to right, J.F. "Hank" Larcombe, Karl M. Knight, Charles "Bud" Havens, and Harry T. Knight Jr., all from the WCC, represented the United States at the 1924 Paris Olympic Games. Note they are holding double-blade paddles, not rowing oars. WCC members had been agitating for paddling events to be part of the Olympics, and the French Olympic Committee, as host of the games, asked the Canadian Canoe Association to demonstrate canoe racing at the games (in Olympic parlance, "canoe" includes both single- and double-blade disciplines). The Canadians in turn invited US participation. Four WCCers made up the entire US contingent, and while the Canadians won all the single-blade events, the WCC swept the double-blade races and came home with three gold, one silver, and two bronze medals. Canoeing became an official Olympic sport at the 1936 Olympic Games in Berlin and has been ever since, thanks in part to WCC advocacy. Twenty-eight WCC paddlers, including seven women, have represented the United States at Olympic Games from 1940 to 1996 (war years excepted), more than any other US canoe club. (Courtesy of WCC.)

SAILING CANOES. During the 1920s and 1930s, sailing canoes, both for relaxation and competition, was a popular pastime at the WCC. Keeping a tippy craft with no keel upright in the wind took considerable skill. While some canoes came equipped for sailing, others required modifications, and sailors, unlike paddlers, spent many hours outfitting and tinkering with their craft. Note the club's owl totem on the sail. (Courtesy of the William "Dusty" Rhodes family.)

A SAILING FLEET. Groups of WCC members would take daylong or multiday tidewater trips in their sailing canoes. Double-masted rigging was just one of many adaptions devised by ingenious sailors. With the advent of World War II, interest in canoe sailing declined, although there are still enthusiasts. Note the extensive run of Dempsey's canoe sheds in the background. The presence of both the Aqueduct Bridge and the Key Bridge places this photograph between 1923 and 1933. (Courtesy of WCC.)

WOMEN'S QUAD. The 1938 *Washington Herald* caption reads, "The Big Four in feminine canoeing ranks of the Capital," introducing a women's paddling foursome preparing for the President's Cup Race in 1938. They are, from left to right, Mary Birch, Margie and Betty Burch, and Mrs. James Burch (the wife of a former commodore of the WCC). The star on their paddle blades indicates that at least some were members of the Potomac Boat Club (PBC); paddlers sometimes moved memberships between the PBC and WCC. (Courtesy of the William "Dusty" Rhodes family.)

WOMEN'S ROLES. Even as they were competing regularly, WCC women continued in support roles: encouraging the men as spectators and helpmates or supervising tasks such as changing the tire of what looks like a 1941 Ford on a WCC road trip. (Courtesy of the William "Dusty" Rhodes family.)

PISTOL IN HAND. The race starter, standing at right, has just lowered his pistol after signaling the start of the 1939 national championship four-man, double-blade race. Unusually, the double-bladers are kneeling rather than sitting. Nine years after the first national canoe championships, this competition was held at the New York World's Fair. Note the fair's parachute drop amusement ride in the background. (Courtesy of Jim Ross.)

THE PRESS. Photographers from the *Washington Post* lean over the edge of the WCC docks to get close-ups of competitors. Newspapers provided extensive coverage of canoe and kayak races as well as crew regattas to a hungry public in the first decades of the 20th century. One canoe race in New York attracted 30,000 spectators. (Courtesy of the William "Dusty" Rhodes family.)

LATTER-DAY KNIGHTS. A popular competition for WCC canoeists was tilting, a take-off on medieval jousting contests. With a canoe (paddled by one person) as his "steed," the tilter would charge his opponent in another canoe and attempt to dislodge him. While originally playful, this competition was not for the faint of heart; often, in addition to bruises, canoeists ended up in the drink. WCC's Bill Havens Jr. (above, right) seems to have the upper hand. Havens (below, right) draws a bead on his opponent during the national tilting championships at the 1939 New York World's Fair as an eager crowd looks on. With his partner William "Dusty" Rhodes, Havens won at least a dozen national tilting crowns. Note the fair's Cyclone roller coaster in the background. (Above, courtesy of WCC; below, courtesy of Jim Ross.)

WORLD WAR II. From left to right at right, WCCers Bud Parker and brothers Bill Havens Jr. and Frank Havens stand in front of the WCC in their Army Air Corps uniforms. Many WCC members had served in the armed forces during the war and came home eager to paddle; they resumed competition without missing a beat. Below, from left to right, Ebby Trilling, Frank Havens, Bill Havens Jr., and William "Dusty" Rhodes were the 1947 national champions in a single-blade four. The Havens brothers moved on to the 1948 Olympics in London, where Frank won a silver medal at 10,000 meters and Bill had a fifth-place finish in the 1,000-meter race. (Right, courtesy of Dan and Bonnie Havens; below, courtesy of WCC.)

GOLD AT HELSINKI, 1952. Using a borrowed paddle, the WCC's Frank Havens captured the gold medal in the 10,000-meter single-blade canoe event at the Helsinki Olympic Games, finishing in the world-record time of 57 minutes, 41 seconds. Havens had broken his three racing paddles while training. In an extraordinary display of sportsmanship, Canadian canoe coach Earl "Doc" Whittall gave Havens his personal paddle for the finals, and that paddle is now on display at the Canadian Canoe Museum. Havens, here at age 28, went on to compete for another 60 years, winning hundreds of races in various disciplines and inspiring multiple generations of WCC paddlers. WCCers have won two of the five gold medals that US canoeists garnered over all Olympic games and accounted for one third of all flatwater Olympic medals ever won by the United States. (Courtesy of Dan and Bonnie Havens.)

OLYMPIC MEDALS. The gold medal (obverse and reverse) won by Frank Havens in Helsinki in 1952 was only the second Olympic medal in canoe or kayak ever won by an American; the first was Havens's silver medal four years earlier in London. Subsequently, two WCC paddlers medaled in 1964 and one in 1988; with Havens, they are among only nine American paddlers to ever to win Olympic medals in flatwater canoe or kayak. (Courtesy of Dan and Bonnie Havens.)

WESTERN UNITED TELEGRAPH CO.
24545 E 92ND STREET
NEW YORK, NEW YORK 20154

FROM: FRANK HAVENS
      HELSINKI GRANDE HOSTEL

TO: MR. BILL HAVENS

      DEAR DAD,
      I'VE HAD A WONDERFULL TIME HERE IN FINLAND COMPETING FOR THE UNITED STATES
      I'M ON MY WAY HOME TODAY. THE 10,000 METER WAS A REAL CHALLENGE,
      LET ME TELL YOU. THE HUNGARIAN AND THE CHECH WERE AHEAD OF ME ALL THE
      WAY, BUT I GAVE IT MY ALL.
      PAPPY, THERE'S SOMETHING ELSE I WANT YOU TO KNOW:
      THANKS FOR STAYING HOME AND WAITING AROUND FOR ME TO BE BORN BACK
      IN 1924. I'M COMING HOME WITH THE GOLD MEDAL YOU SHOULD HAVE WON.
      YOUR LOVING SON,
      FRANK.

TELEGRAM HOME. After winning the gold medal, Frank Havens sent this telegram to his father, Bill Havens Sr., who, despite being the foremost single-blade paddler in the country at the time, had foregone the 1924 Olympics in order to be home for the birth of Frank. (Courtesy of Dan and Bonnie Havens.)

PRESIDENTIAL HONOR. In June 1953, the WCC's gold medal–winner Frank Havens (first row, far left) was among 44 of the America's leading athletes honored by Pres. Dwight D. Eisenhower at a White House Sports Champions luncheon. Others in the front row include, from left to right, four-star general Alfred Gruenther (in uniform, a famous bridge player and partner of the president's), baseball hall-of-famers Tris Speaker and Clark Griffith, President Eisenhower, tennis legend (and lieutenant commander) Helen Hull Jacobs, and golfer Gene Sarazen. Heavyweight boxing champion Rocky Marciano (looking to the side, in dark suit) is behind Sarazen. Other well-known athletes in attendance included African American Olympic gold medalist Norvell Lee, track star Arthur Bragg, and swimmer Mary Freeman. Baseball icon Joe DiMaggio was present but is not in the photograph. Following lunch, the group joined the president at the 1953 Congressional baseball game. (Courtesy of Eisenhower Presidential Library.)

OLYMPIC PRIDE. WCC club president Joseph S. Mawson (on the right in dark pants) and Bill Havens Jr. raise the Olympic flag at the WCC after club members Frank Havens and Bill Schuette returned from 1952 Helsinki Olympic Games. Frank stands shirtless with his son Dan on his shoulders. Older brother Bill was also a standout paddler, winning national championships in five different disciplines from the 1930s to the 1950s. But for World War II and a freak accident, Bill would likely have qualified for five consecutive Olympic teams. Below, Frank Havens (wearing one of his many race participation medals) continued to compete into his 80s and paddled a kayak daily until near his 94th birthday. He died in 2018. (Right, courtesy of WCC; below, courtesy of Dan and Bonnie Havens.)

A First for Women. Ruth DeForrest poses with Frank Havens at the 1952 US Olympic team trials. Ruth excelled at the trials (which included women's kayak events for the first time), winning all of her races and becoming the first US woman to qualify for the Olympics in kayak. But the qualification was retracted by the US national governing body for canoe/kayak due to disagreements about training, budgets, and chaperones, which many saw as (then legal) gender discrimination, and Ruth was not permitted to go with the team to Helsinki. Soon after her Olympic disappointment, Ruth moved to California, married (becoming a Colley), raised a family, and became a champion tennis player and golfer. Almost 50 years later, Frank Havens convinced her to team up with him at the 1998 Nike World Masters Games (below) at Lake Vancouver, Washington, where they won numerous medals. According to Ruth, the two-piece bathing suit she wore in 1952 "was considered risqué but it was great for paddling." (Both, courtesy of WCC.)

Five

COMPETITION AND CRAFT FROM 1960 TO 2019

The 1960s brought major changes to paddle sports, and the WCC was at the forefront. While WCC men continued to compete at the highest level, the decade was a breakthrough for women. WCC female paddlers were a dominant presence in double-blade (kayak) events nationally and, beginning in 1960, were on the US Olympic team continuously through 1996. Ten years before Title IX of the Education Amendments of 1972, which put women on more equal footing with men, WCC women had racing success and coaching roles in what had previously been exclusive male domains.

But the WCC was behind the times in some ways. Women were not given full WCC membership until the late 1960s, a full 25 years after the American Canoe Association had taken this step. And it was not until 1986 that the WCC had its first (and still its only) female president.

The craft being raced by both men and women were also changing, as faster boats with innovative designs and lighter materials (such as molded plywood, fiberglass, and later Kevlar and carbon fiber) became available. Improved training regimes contributed to greater speed and faster times. Globalization, too, played a role. US and Canadian boat design have cross-fertilized since the 19th century but, beginning around 1950, Europe became a leader in cutting-edge designs like the Max Anderson kayaks from Sweden and Denmark's Struer boats.

Since 1960, WCC athletes have paddled throughout the United States and on four continents; in Europe alone, they have raced in two dozen countries. Competing at distances from 200 meters to 260 miles and paddling solo, tandem, or in teams of up to 20 paddlers in dragon boats, WCC men and women have won championships in more than a dozen paddling disciplines, including sprint canoe, kayak, outrigger, dragon boat, marathon canoe, and stand-up paddleboard. Women have been global leaders in the fight for Olympic equity, and for the first time, the 2020 Olympics in Tokyo will include women's sprint canoe events.

The competitive spirit and human ingenuity will always find new outlets. The Hawaiian surfboard evolved to become the now popular stand-up paddleboard (SUP), super-light canoes were built for long-distance races, and innovative "surf skis" have provided another swift option for racers. But the hard work of propelling a boat with a paddle has never really changed.

LAST HURRAH. Four WCC paddlers, (front to back) Steve Ainsley, Roy Jobber, Andy Weigand, and Mike Ainsley, used the traditional lightweight wooden quad to win the C-4 National Championship in 1967. This may have been the last major race won in this boat, as new designs and synthetic materials were already well on their way to replacing these beautiful all-wood craft. (Courtesy of WCC.)

NEW BOATS, NEW PADDLERS. Two unidentified women in the 1950s carry a new Swedish-designed Max Anderson kayak up the WCC ramp. In the 1960s, some WCC members began building their own boats out of fiberglass. Note the rowing shells in the background and the cars on the recently opened George Washington Memorial Parkway across the river. The picture predates the high-rises in Rosslyn, Virginia, that dominate the skyline today. (Courtesy of WCC.)

CHANGE AGENT: GLORIANE PERRIER. Arriving from Lewiston, Maine, in the late 1950s to work as a secretary at the Army Signal Corps, "Glo" was introduced to kayak paddling after her powerful heaves of a bowling ball attracted the notice of a member of the WCC's bowling team. Glo almost immediately became a paddling standout (she also excelled at softball and speed skating) and was the first American female kayaker to go to the Olympics (Rome, 1960). She was the national ladies single kayak (K-1) champion in 1960 and 1961 and teamed up to win an Olympic silver medal in 1964. Because she had famously poor balance in a solo boat, she usually paddled tandem and was five times national champion in double kayak (K-2). Glo went on to win many races nationally and internationally and, as a coach, to teach and inspire a generation of women paddlers until her retirement in 1983; during her tenure, every US Olympic team included WCC women. Always adventurous, Glo taught herself to ride a Harley Davidson at age 73 and made two cross-country trips. (Courtesy of DCPL, WCC Collection.)

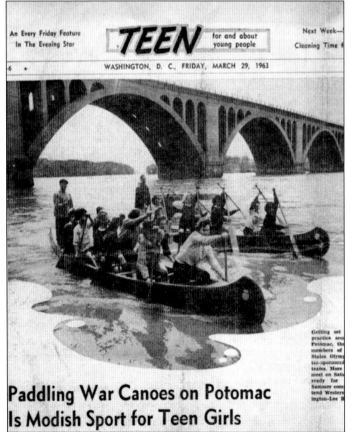

An Every Friday Feature
In The Evening Star

TEEN

for and about
young people

Next Week—
Cleaning Time f

WASHINGTON, D. C., FRIDAY, MARCH 29, 1963

Getting set
practice ses
Potomac, the
members of
States Olym
ics-sponsore
teams. More
meet on Satu
ready for
Summer com
tend Western
ington-Lee H

Paddling War Canoes on Potomac Is Modish Sport for Teen Girls

TEAM PADDLING. WCC men (here in 1936) had competed in war canoes carrying 6–15 paddlers from the club's beginning. But it was a novel sport for women. In 1962, the US Olympic Committee for the first time sponsored young women to train and race and placed war canoes at the WCC and the Potomac Boat Club for beginners to improve technique and teamwork. At left, in 1963, enthusiastic high schoolers from Western High School in DC and Washington and Lee in Virginia learn the essentials of paddling. Said one participant: "It's a good sport for girls to get interested in . . . especially to meet boys." (Above, courtesy of WCC; left, courtesy of the William "Dusty" Rhodes family.)

CHANGING ROLES. Debby Smith (later Debby Page) started paddling in 1961 at age 13 and soon became part of a group of elite WCC women kayakers who raced throughout the United States and Europe. Later, her jobs took her away from DC for extended periods, but when possible, she returned to the WCC to coach. Starting in 2009, Smith focused her support on paracanoe events for paddlers with disabilities; these events are now part of the quadrennial Paralympics, and Debby is the team leader for the 2020 Olympic Games. (Courtesy of WCC.)

PADDLER/COACH. Charlie Lundmark, born of Swedish American parents, had the distinction of representing two nations at the Olympic Games—as an alternate for Sweden in 1952 and as a sprint kayaker for the US in 1960. A US kayak champion, Lundmark went on to a successful coaching career, and he was both coach and manager of the US canoe team at the 1972 Munich Olympic Games. He also served in many leadership roles at WCC. Skilled coaching has been crucial to WCC paddling success for a century. (Courtesy of WCC.)

TEEN CHAMP. Seventh-grader Francine Fox was playing tag on her junior high school playground when fellow student Debby Smith suggested she try paddling. Fox, then 13, made a sensational entry into the racing world in 1962, besting her coach Glo Perrier after only six months of paddling to become the national kayak champion. She later became a schoolteacher but continued winning races (for the WCC and then the Potomac Boat Club) until 1974, earning two Olympic berths and a silver medal (with Glo Perrier) before retiring, marrying, and raising a family. She was the WCC's second celebrity paddler (after Olympian Frank Havens), and the press became obsessed with the attractive teenager, following her life on and off the river. Newspaper accounts of Fox and other female paddlers routinely called them "girls" and used descriptors like "comely," "pretty," and "winsome;" there were no parallel comments about men! (Both, courtesy of *Washington Star* Collection, copyright *Washington Post*, reprinted with permission of DCPL.)

OLYMPIC SUCCESS. Gloriane "Glo" Perrier (left) and Francine Fox (right) combined their talents (Glo's power and Francine's finesse) to capture the silver medal at the 1964 Tokyo Olympics in the 500-meter tandem kayak race. They, along with Marcia Jones Smoke (who won a bronze medal), were the first and, to date, only US women to have medaled in Olympic kayak competition, and *Life* magazine covered their accomplishment. Training workouts were "intense, long, and the men's group did not wait for stragglers," said Fox. (Courtesy of WCC.)

NEXT GENERATION OLYMPIANS. What may look like a glamorous Hollywood after-party is actually a group of US Olympic kayakers assembled for a pre-Olympic workout in 1972 at the ship testing tank of a high-security US Navy facility, the David Taylor Model Basin in suburban Maryland. Pictured are, from left to right, (first row) Charlie Lundmark (coach) and Captain Nelson, a Navy official; (second row) Jerry Welborne, Nancy Purves, Linda Dragan, Al Whitney, and Phil Rogosheske; (third row) Jack Brosius and Steve Kelly. All but Kelly, Welborne, and Rogosheske were from the WCC. (Courtesy of Nancy Purves.)

"Tootsie Rollers." Elite WCC kayakers during the 1970s included, from left to right, Jackie Scribner, Nancy Purves, Theresa DiMarino, and Linda Dragan. Nicknamed the "Tootsie Rollers," they were 1978 national champions in the 500-meter four-person kayak (below). All but Jackie Scribner represented the United States at Olympic Games between 1972 and 1988. Theresa DiMarino (married name Haught), still paddling at the WCC after 50 years (as of 2019), began kayaking at age 11 when WCC legend Gloriane Perrier recruited her and other youths at the Mount Vernon Yacht Club. By age 16, DiMarino was competing internationally and was twice selected for Olympic teams. (Above, courtesy of WCC; below, courtesy of Nancy Purves.)

HIGH KNEEL/SPRINT FOR WOMEN. The WCC's Sue Wolpert (above) paddles with Dan Havens in a canoe race in Baltimore around 1980. Her powerful strokes in this Olympic-style position earned her the nickname "Sue Canoe." Several times Wolpert raced in a major competition with a male partner, only to be disqualified after officials realized "S. Wolpert" was female. It was not until 2000 that women were permitted to compete in high-kneel (sprint canoe) events at the US National Championships . . . and then, against the men. In 2002, USA Canoe/Kayak officially added women-only events. The WCC's Pam Boteler (below, left), the first woman to compete in sprint canoe at the US National Championships and a leading advocate for gender equality in Olympic canoeing, teamed with Itzel Reza (right), a former Olympic kayaker for Mexico, in a tandem sprint canoe (C-2) at the 2010 World Championships. Women's canoe events will debut at the 2020 Tokyo Olympics. (Above, courtesy of Dan and Bonnie Havens; below, courtesy of Brian K. Donnelly.)

WHITEWATER TRADITION. Two WCC members negotiate rapids near Old Anglers Inn, perhaps during the annual 7.5-mile Potomac River Race ending at Sycamore Island. Athletes at the WCC have usually focused on competitive flatwater canoe and kayak events that are competed for nationally and in the Olympic Games. But starting with its founders, WCCers have also enjoyed taking on the challenges of the abundant whitewater on the Potomac and in nearby states. (Courtesy of DCPL, Washingtoniana Collection.)

To Mary Garland
With best wishes, G Bush

TWO PRESIDENTS. Mary Garland was the WCC's first (and only) woman president (1986–1988 and again in 1993). Garland was greeted by Pres. George H.W. Bush and Barbara Bush ("I wasn't alone, there were about 1,000 other guests," she admitted) at a White House reception for the 1992 Olympic team. After years of racing in both whitewater and flatwater, Garland served in many national leadership roles for paddle sports, including team leader for sprint canoe/kayak at the 1992 Olympics. (Courtesy of Mary Garland.)

EQUITY FOR WOMEN. Beginning in the 1920s, the WCC encouraged and supported women who wanted to paddle and compete; Elizabeth Smith teamed with Harry Knight Jr. for many races. By 1950, international competition for women paddlers had become the norm, and women were full members of the American Canoe Association. But in 1952, the WCC's Ruth DeForrest was denied a place on the US Olympic team by the sport's governing body (see page 66). In the 1960s, society (and the WCC) opened new opportunities for women; the club agreed to full membership for women for the first time, and the WCC's female athletes were very successful at the national and Olympic levels and as coaches. In recent decades, individual women competitors and teams, in every paddling discipline, have been fully equal to the men in both numbers of participants and success in competition. Below, Kathleen McNamee and Dan Havens race the Adirondack 90-miler in 2015. (Above, courtesy of WCC; below, courtesy of Bonnie Havens.)

WAR CANOES. Long a Canadian tradition, war canoes became part of the WCC's fleet around 1915, when the club acquired a wooden Peterborough war canoe. With 15 paddlers, the boat was swift, and the WCC won many races on the Potomac. After the WCC (and other clubs) could not field teams, the 15-man boat was sold. But at the same time (early 1960s), the US Olympic Committee sent three 9-person Old Town war canoes to the Potomac River to enhance training and teamwork for aspiring athletes. These canoes have been in use ever since, although they have needed major refurbishing from time to time. War canoe racing on the East Coast tapered off in the 1980s as other team paddling craft (like outriggers and dragon boats) became popular. Recently, the WCC canoes have been used primarily during winter months for group training and fun (below). (Above, courtesy of Dan and Bonnie Havens; below, courtesy of Steve Ball.)

DRAGON BOATS. In the early 1990s, with Matt Butcher as steersman (far left) and Dave Armstrong (right) drumming a cadence up front, the WCC women's dragon boat team churns up the Potomac. With 10 women paddlers on a side, the heavy craft are raced extensively in the Far East, and the WCC team traveled to Thailand and other countries to compete. The team moved to an Anacostia River location in the mid-1990s. (Courtesy of Marcie Pacilli Moline.)

OUTRIGGER. The WCC team of, from left to right, Mitch Potter, Quincy Ayscue, Matt West, Andrey Drachenko, Blaise Rhodes, and Martin Lowenfish crash the surf during the East Coast Outrigger Racing Association (ECORA) race at Sandbridge, Virginia, in 2006. An import from Hawaii, outrigger paddling became a favorite competitive sport at the WCC for both men and women in the late 1990s after the club acquired its first two OC-6 (six-person) boats. The men's and women's teams travel to Hawaii each year to compete. (Courtesy of John Bekerman.)

EVOLUTION OF BOATS. To improve speed, paddle craft have gotten narrower over the years; the solo high-kneel sprint canoe (called a C-1) is now only 10 inches wide. Pictured are some current (2019) state-of-the-art designs; from left to right are the marathon canoe, OC-1 (solo outrigger), C-1, surf ski, K-1 (solo kayak), and two more C-1s. In the background are a tandem kayak and a stand-up paddleboard. Six of the pictured paddlers are products of the WCC Juniors program. (Courtesy of Mary Rollefson.)

SUP. Born out of surfing, stand-up paddling (SUP) was formally introduced in the DC area by WCC member Kathy Summers in 2008. Its popularity has grown exponentially since. SUP paddlers can enjoy solitary, mindful paddling, running rapids, or racing on flat or whitewater. An accomplished competitor, Summers has taught hundreds of novices to paddle and has helped develop the safety protocols for SUP that are used today. (Courtesy of Steve Fisher.)

JUNIORS. The WCC has engaged young paddlers in the art of canoeing since its founding, and by the 1960s, the club was actively recruiting and training youth. Here, a youngster (without a life jacket!) learns the art of high-kneel paddling from his dad in the 1930s. The background structure may be Warner's Canoe House, which collapsed in the 1936 flood and was never rebuilt. (Courtesy of WCC.)

SUPPORTING CAST FOR KIDS. With the arrival of Vitaly Bednov (far left) as the WCC Juniors coach in 1990, what had been a modest program for novices took off, and several of the club's elite paddlers pitched in to coach. Next to Bednov is former national champion Roy Jobber, and on the far right are Olympian Jack Brosius and longtime coach Debby Page. WCC Juniors have participated in national and international races since the 1960s, building the foundation for continuing WCC preeminence in paddle sports. (Courtesy of Blaise Rhodes.)

CHALLENGING THE YOUNG. WCC Juniors coach Kathleen McNamee (on right) teaches seventh-grader Aida Gill the art of high-kneel (sprint) canoeing in 2014. Junior paddlers are quickly exposed to fast but initially unstable canoes and kayaks, and swims are frequent. Below, an unidentified young paddler gets "baptized." Kathleen started paddling in the WCC Juniors program and became accomplished in several disciplines; she is the latest in a long line of WCC women to coach both juniors and adults. (Both, courtesy of WCC.)

SUMMER CAMPS. Throughout the 1990s, the year-round WCC Juniors paddling program was augmented with a summer camp. In addition to a great deal of paddling and swimming, campers learned about the ecology of the Potomac River; here, they use nets to seine for small fish and macro-invertebrates. (Courtesy of WCC.)

TRAINING BY CHAMPIONS. The 2002 WCC Juniors team poses with coaches Mike and Alexandra Harbold (left) and Debby Page (far right). The Harbolds, who joined the WCC in the late 1980s, are highly decorated paddlers who brought their experience in international competition and as multitime Olympians to the youth. Mike was a Pan American Games gold medalist. During the Harbolds' decade-long tenure, WCC Junior paddlers were regularly named to the US Junior World Championship team and frequently came home with medals from the US national championships. (Courtesy of Dan and Bonnie Havens.)

To Bill,
The best coach I could have asked for! I couldn't have done it without you.

Norman Bellingham

A Second Olympic Gold. Formerly a whitewater boater from Bethesda, Maryland, the WCC's Norman Bellingham (left) turned to flatwater kayak in 1983. After five years of intense competition and training, he teamed with Greg Barton (right) to capture the gold medal in the kayak (K-2) 500-meter race at the 1988 Seoul Olympic Games. The winning duo used a cutting-edge kayak designed by a team that included a fellow WCC member. It was the second gold medal and fourth Olympic medal overall for the WCC in its history. Bellingham won numerous world championship and Pan American Championship medals during his career and went on to become a senior official with the US Olympic Committee. He signed this photograph for his coach, Bill Endicott, who served for many years as coach of the US whitewater team. Since 1996, no WCCers have been on Olympic teams, due in part to international rule changes that made gaining an Olympic berth considerably more challenging for athletes from all countries. (Courtesy of Bill and Abbie Endicott.)

CHALLENGE IN TEXAS. In 2012, the WCC's two-time champion Andrew Soles (in the third position from left) is joined by five teammates, including WCCers Andrew Stephens (in the bow) and Sam Ritchie (in fourth position) to win the 260-mile Texas Water Safari race in 38.5 hours . . . three hours ahead of the second-place finishers. Although no longer the longest marathon canoe race in the country, the Texas Water Safari (from San Marcos, Texas, to the Gulf of Mexico) set the standard for "ultra-marathon" paddling when it started in 1963. Boats with as many as six paddlers are allowed on the winding river course. Below, the 2019 team portages its canoe past a waterfall, one of many hazards on the challenging route. (Both, courtesy of John Russell.)

INSPIRATION FOR JUNIORS. WCC outrigger paddlers, both young and mature, assembled at the Hoe Wa'a Challenge in Atlantic City in 2018. The WCC fielded three women's teams, one of which finished first overall, and the club had the only juniors team in the race. In the back row, at far left, is the team's coach, Kelly Rhodes, who has led women's outrigger at the WCC for two decades as well as winning individual championships in multiple paddling disciplines. This intergenerational group provides great inspiration for the next crop of athletes. (Courtesy of Bonnie Havens.)

Six

Club Traditions

By the time the Washington Canoe Club was founded in 1904, canoeing was already a popular national pastime, and boating clubs were a well-established part of the Washington scene. Since the establishment of the city's first rowing associations in the 1840s, river enthusiasts had joined to form over a dozen clubs, many with their own boathouses. Beginning in the 1860s, the Georgetown waterfront became the locus for both rowing and paddling; several new boathouses were built. The WCC's founders, however, sought a club focused exclusively on canoeing, with a strong bent for competition, and the WCC was dedicated from the start to "the art of paddling."

But the club quickly became much more. It built bodies and camaraderie through participation in many sports. The WCC boasted at least eight of its own teams to compete in everything from swimming and track to wrestling and bowling. It hosted dinners, dances, oyster roasts, and crab feasts in addition to its regattas. It put on theatricals, masquerades, and operettas (some involving half the club membership, who wrote both the music and librettos). Minstrel shows—so popular then, so inappropriate and offensive now—were also part of the fare. The WCC involved whole families in a wide range of recreational activities, four seasons a year, with paddling, fishing, swimming, and camping during the summer and skating in the winter. The WCC was the place to congregate, enjoy each other's company, work (for the WCC boathouse was a never-ending do-it-yourself project), and compete. But it was also a place for frequent fun, mischief, and high jinx. Members vacationed together in places like Sugar Island, on the St. Lawrence River in Ontario, Canada; the club became a large extended family. By the 1920s, newspapers were calling DC the nation's canoeing capital, and the WCC was at the center. But busy as it was, the club also offered a respite and a place to temporarily slow down for the club's city dwellers.

Was the WCC as a social institution unique? Perhaps no more than any other such group. But one senses, in the robustness of member loyalty, the great variety of club activities, and the manifest "work hard, play hard" ethic that has persisted for over a century, a distinctive spirit and record that makes this club special.

Boating on the Potomac River, Washington. D. C. At Aqueduct Bridge Leading to Arlington and Fort Myer, Va.

EARLY PADDLERS. Canoeing was already a popular leisure activity on the Potomac River in Washington (and many other cities) by the time of the WCC's founding in 1904. At least five Georgetown boathouses catered to renters or were headquarters for clubs that supported canoeing. The Aqueduct Bridge in the background and the dress of the paddlers dates this postcard to around 1900. (Courtesy of Jerry A. McCoy.)

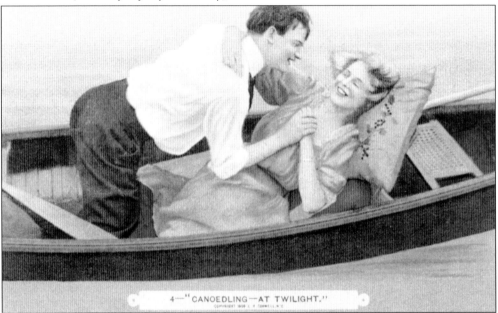

4—"CANOEDLING—AT TWILIGHT."

A CANOEING DATE. Canoes provided peace and privacy, which could be hard to find for courting couples, even as America moved beyond the Victorian era in the early 1900s. Social conventions still dictated restraint and decorum; in puritanical Boston at the time, kissing and lying together in canoes were punishable offenses. The gentleman in this postcard seems willing to risk the penalties, though, to steal a kiss from an apparently willing partner. (Courtesy of John Summers.)

Transportation to the WCC. Streetcars and trolleys were one of the best ways for WCC members and guests to reach the canoe club from the downtown business district (here, the intersection of Fifteenth and G Streets in northwest DC). The Georgetown Car Barn, only a few hundred yards from the WCC, was a major hub, and trolleys ran across the Aqueduct Bridge, providing the connection to Virginia as well. (Courtesy of the Historical Society of Washington, DC.)

Swimming, c. 1930. Summer meant swimming in the refreshing Potomac River. Even as pollution levels rose in the mid-20th century, WCC members continued to jump in. The early club had its own float, and swimming and diving competitions were common. The photograph captures what appears to be the start of a swim race. (Courtesy of WCC.)

Tad Rutherford

A PLACE FOR KIDS. Tad Rutherford, possibly the child of WCC master paddler Reginald Rutherford, poses in a WCC jersey in this 1920s photograph. The WCC has been a family place since its beginning and a great place for kids to find adventure beside the river, on it, and in it. A life preserver sits on the ramp behind Tad. (Courtesy of WCC.)

FLIPS. Exuberant youngsters practice their flips off the WCC dock. After the decades of poor water quality and negative press coverage (especially in the 1950s and 1960s), multiple jurisdictions coordinated to upgrade upstream sewage treatment facilities, and with a number of new federal laws in place, the river became noticeably cleaner by the late 1970s. (Courtesy of WCC.)

FAMILY OUTINGS. The WCC's Paxton Baker introduces five children to canoeing around 2014. The Potomac River in front of the club is a wonderful place for youth to learn the basics of paddling and to get comfortable in boats. Note that everyone in the boat is wearing a life vest. (Courtesy of Blaise Rhodes.)

SWAMPED CANOE. Under controlled conditions, WCC children learn what to do after a tip-over: stay calm, stick with the canoe, bail if possible, and swim the boat to shore. The wet dock suggests that many of the kids have participated in this exercise. (Courtesy of WCC.)

WINTERTIME FUN. WCC members use shovels to clear trails and a small rink for skating on the frozen, snow-covered Potomac in front of the WCC. The steep banks of Rosslyn, Virginia, appear in the background, prior to the construction of the George Washington Memorial Parkway. The section of the parkway above the Key Bridge to Spout Run, including along the shore directly across from the WCC, was completed in the late 1940s. (Courtesy of WCC.)

PICK-UP HOCKEY, PRE-1920. WCC member Reginald Rutherford eagerly awaits others to join him in a game of hockey; it appears that it is not just the river that is frozen. And in case there are no takers for the hockey, Rutherford has a canoe at the ready. (Courtesy of WCC.)

FAMILY AFFAIR. Skating out from the WCC (background), this group of 10 skaters is about to "crack the whip" (pivoting the line to give the outermost skaters a thrilling ride). Dempsey's Boathouse and the Key Bridge arches are downriver of the WCC, and the tower of the Georgetown Car Barn is on the hill. (Courtesy of WCC.)

WHEELS ON ICE, c. 1995. This training bicycle (with the Key Bridge arches in the background) is not the only wheeled vehicle to ever have ventured onto the frozen Potomac. A *Washington Herald* account from 1912 tells of two daredevils driving their car out on the ice from the Virginia shore and towing lines of skaters up and down the river at speeds of up to 40 miles per hour. The subheading on the article—"Several Close Calls"—would seem to be stating the obvious. (Courtesy of Mike and Alexandra Harbold.)

Work Parties. WCC crew use an improvised crane to swing one of the ramps leading down to the dock into place. Up and down the river, docks and ramps are typically removed for the winter months to prevent damage from ice and floods and then reinstalled in the spring. Note the narrow porch along the front of the boathouse, which was the main outdoor sitting area until the concrete apron was laid around 1970. (Courtesy of WCC.)

Dock Floats. Early on, empty whiskey casks were used as floats for the docks. A barrel would be filled with water, pushed under the dock, the water hand-pumped out, and a plug hammered in to seal it. Old-timers remember the sweet smell of the empty casks. Here, a champion WCC tilter takes a break to practice his balance on a barrel. (Courtesy of the William "Dusty" Rhodes family.)

HIGH WIRE ACTS. Upkeep of the WCC has been a never-ending project since the boathouse was built, and volunteering has been a hallmark of the club's members. Here, club painters are at work in 1946. A close examination of the acrobatic WCC member on the flagpole (right) reveals he is safely suspended in a boatswain's chair. (Both, courtesy of WCC.)

BEER. From left to right, club members Bill Snow, Gil Lagorse, Don Miller, and Karl Knight have a beer at the Grill Room bar. WCC athletes have traditionally taken time for a drink after a strenuous training session. The large beer containers may be pitchers to serve others or a throwback to the huge mugs in the cartoon mural of early WCC members, seen on the wall above the men. (Courtesy of WCC.)

SUMMER CRAB FEAST, C. 1955. A crowd on the narrow deck of the WCC boathouse cracks piles of crabs with hammers and washes them down with glasses of beer. Club members and guests have enjoyed the bounty of the tidal Potomac and Chesapeake Bay since the beginning, with fresh crabs readily available during the summer season. (Courtesy of the William "Dusty" Rhodes family.)

WINTER OYSTER ROAST, 2008. The WCC's Jim Ross shovels steaming oysters over the fire at a 2008 wintertime oyster roast as Roy Jobber assists and Linda Ross looks on. The freedom to cook out by the river over an open fire (contained in a fire pit) is a time-honored tradition and is prized by the club. (Courtesy of Blaise Rhodes.)

Theatricals. A major club-wide undertaking in the WCC's first years was to put on plays and operettas. Some took place on the small stage in the WCC ballroom, others at local theaters like the one above; note the violin in the orchestra pit (foreground). For major shows, half the club membership (then numbering about 100) would perform, write the scripts and scores, or serve as stagehands. No information could be found about this club production of *Divine Diana Logan*. (Courtesy of the William "Dusty" Rhodes family.)

Lively Social Life. Dinners, receptions, dances with live music (here, New Year's Eve around 1960), "ladies' nights," and masquerades were monthly events at the WCC; the spacious ballroom, with its balcony looking out onto the river, provided a romantic venue. A typical dance evening ran from 10:00 p.m. to 2:00 a.m. (Courtesy of Dan and Bonnie Havens.)

WATER CARNIVAL. In early years, the WCC held a Bar Club Regatta, featuring slapstick competitions like this stand-up race; other contests had participants in rocking chairs, bouncing on canoe gunwales, or paddling with their hands in swamped canoes. One boy has a good perch on the club's high diving board, and others are closely following the action on the edge of the dock. The large tower across the river is presumably anchoring cables used during the construction of the Key Bridge, dating this photograph to around 1922. Note that many of the men wear swim tops. Men's swimwear included a jersey to cover their chests, as it was illegal (and considered indecent) in most states and cities for men to go topless, even at the beach. Not until protracted legal battles and civil disobedience in the 1930s was this societal prohibition lifted. (Courtesy of WCC.)

HANGING OUT. One way to while away the hours at the canoe club was to join one of the frequent card games. Here, WCC members John "Fats" Shugrue (left), Dick Ackad (right), and an unidentified third player (center), fortified with their bottles, pass the time in the Grill Room. Members would also gather around the large radio to listen to their favorite show or the ball game. (Courtesy of WCC.)

"FORE." The WCC dock has seen many competitions over the years, but the club never fielded a golf team. Nonetheless, this 1920s postcard shows a duffer about to tee off and try to clear a significant water hazard: the Potomac River. The reference on the card inscription—"Alien has lived in this country for many years but has never applied for citizenship papers"—is lost to history. (Courtesy of WCC.)

AN ELUSIVE FIGURE, C. 1925. In the center of the dock in a newsboy hat, amidst the flags marking a major holiday or regatta, is Pembroke Smith. There is no known close-up photograph of Pembroke (or "Pemmy" as he was affectionately known). Part African American, part Native American, Pembroke took on the club's paid custodial position in 1912 and served for 41 years until his death at age 90 in 1953. As the club steward, his handyman duties included assisting members with boats, cleaning up the clubhouse, serving as night watchman and guard during floods, and, as stated in his obituary in the September 10, 1953, *Washington Evening Star*, "[helping] members on and off with their coats and wishing them good luck in their race . . . from his favorite chair." Less than five feet in stature, he was a tireless worker and a sometime drinking companion. Club members described Pemmy as "beloved," and he helped make the WCC a community. The long *Star* obituary said he was born in Frederick, Maryland, the son of a Cherokee father; club legend has it that he was born a slave. (Courtesy of WCC.)

CELEBRATIONS. To welcome home WCC's participants in the 1924 Olympic games in Paris, the club prepared an elaborate, horse-drawn float. Wives and lady friends in white sailor suits filled the canoe; male club members marched beside with flags and paddles in a parade from Union Station to the canoe club. The decked-out canoes (below) may have been for a 1909 lantern parade, reported in the press as a half-mile line of 100 canoes "brilliantly lighted with Japanese lanterns". The swastika on the bow of one canoe referenced the ornamentation Native American tribes had historically used on their bark canoes. The Old Town Canoe Company offered the swastika as an option for the bow decoration in the early 20th century. The symbol was of course adopted by the Nazi party in the 1920s and has ever since been a symbol of hatred and racial bias. (Both, courtesy of WCC.)

FIVE GENERATIONS OF HAVENS. Maizie Havens (above, left), wife of Frank "Cap" Havens, was the mother of three boys and three girls around the turn of the 20th century. "Cap" Havens owned the Havens Ice and Coal Company in Rosslyn, Virginia; family lore has it that his sons developed their extraordinarily powerful physiques delivering heavy blocks of ice. One son, William D. "Pappy" Havens Sr. (above, right) joined the WCC in 1918 and by the mid-1920s was considered the foremost Olympic-style canoeist in the country. His wife, Ruby, next to him, started as a diver and champion swimmer but became a competitive canoeist as well. Below, from left to right, great-great-grandson Sean, grandson Frank, and great-grandson Dan have all excelled in paddling events, including Olympic sprint canoe, marathon canoe, and outrigger. Others in the wider Havens clan have also been standout paddlers at the WCC as well as national leaders in canoe sports. (All, courtesy of Dan and Bonnie Havens.)

THREE-GENERATION WCC LEGACIES. Above, the family of William "Dusty" Rhodes (who joined the WCC in 1933 and was a national champion canoeist) poses at a 2019 regatta. His wife, Ursula (second row, left), is pictured with an all-star group of paddlers. From left to right are (first row) grandchildren Erin, Sam, Anna, and Luke Rhodes; (second row) son Will; Luke's fiancée, Becca Pinkus; son Blaise; and Blaise's wife, Kelly. All have won multiple championships in craft ranging from kayak and outrigger to sprint and marathon canoe. Larry Schuette (below, left), paddling with Blaise Rhodes in 1986, is the son of two-time Olympian Bill Schuette. Both Larry and Blaise have competed internationally, and following suit, their daughters (below right, from left to right) Helen Schuette, Erin Rhodes, and Becca Schuette competed at the 2019 Olympic Hopes Regatta in Slovakia. (Above and below, left, courtesy of Blaise Rhodes; below, right, courtesy of Becca Schuette.)

HIGHLY COMPETITIVE. The WCC's athletes were not content just to paddle. The WCC track squad, pictured above around 1920, was just one of the teams the club fielded. Others included football and baseball, bowling and basketball, sailing, swimming, shooting, water polo, and wrestling. Members also competed in tennis and boxing, and several excelled in multiple sports. The WCC track team participated in the Penn Relays and other meets; Harry Knight Jr., part of the WCC's foursome that went to the 1924 Olympic Games in Paris, sits in the first row, second from left, wearing his track spikes. Below, members of the WCC football club take the field; helmets were apparently optional. One account from 1920 describes a call for 40 WCC members to come out to take on the Potomac Boat Club's gridiron team at that club's annual oyster roast on Analostan (now Roosevelt) Island. (Both, courtesy of WCC.)

WCC Swim Team. Women, too, enjoyed competition, not only in paddling but also in swimming and diving. This photograph dates from the 1920s. The woman on the far left was Josephine Havens, second wife of William Havens Sr. (Courtesy of Dan and Bonnie Havens.)

The Log. Club news was published monthly in a lively newsletter called the *Log* for 90 years (1916–c. 2007), and for much of that time, the editor and illustrator was William "Dusty" Rhodes. His *Log* covers, cartoons, and writing spanned 60 years and captured the many moods and events of the club year. In recent years, the club has had an electronic newsletter illustrated with color photographs. (Courtesy of the William "Dusty" Rhodes family.)

WATERGATE CONCERTS. On the river side of the Lincoln Memorial are the original Watergate Steps leading down to the Potomac. Beginning in the summer of 1935 and continuing for 30 years (except for a break during World War II), a large barge (far left) was anchored with its stage facing the steps. The National Symphony Orchestra would perform evening concerts for an audience sitting on the steps and for boaters (including WCCers) who snuggled in their canoes after paddling downriver. Pres. Franklin D. Roosevelt attended on occasion, and Frank Sinatra was a featured singer for one performance. In 1965, the concerts were discontinued as noise from the National Airport increased and the barge fell into disrepair. (Both, courtesy of DCPL, Washingtoniana collection.)

SUGAR ISLAND RESPITE. For many WCC members, Sugar Island, lying just off the Canadian shore in the St. Lawrence River and owned by the American Canoe Association, was a favorite getaway for family summer vacation. The island offered some cabins but mostly rustic camping. An annual two-week encampment was the central focus of the summer for families from all over the Eastern Seaboard, and many new friendships were formed. The rendezvouses, too, built an enduring sense of national community and purpose among canoeists. After active days of swimming, paddling, and sailing canoes, folks gathered around a campfire for socializing and singing. Many WCC members have memories of their magical visits to Sugar Island, and a number of families still make the annual pilgrimage. (Both, courtesy of WCC.)

GENERAL CLINTON RACE. Each Memorial Day since 2006, more than 40 WCC members have driven seven hours to participate in the General Clinton Regatta on the Susquehanna River in Oneonta, New York. The WCC team celebrates the life of club member Mitch Madruga, a US Navy veteran who perished in an accident on the Potomac in Washington while training for the regatta in 2006. Up to nine mixed teams of WCC paddlers, using standard recreational aluminum canoes, take on canoeists from across the eastern United States and Canada in a 36-mile, five-leg relay race. The following day, a few well-conditioned and ambitious WCC paddlers enter (and finish) a 70-mile marathon on the river; one resolute club member, Herb Howe, has completed the 70-miler a remarkable 25 times. The weekend pilgrimage and competition build great club camaraderie, and the General Clinton Regatta has become a major milestone each year for the club. This photograph is from 2013. (Courtesy of Linda Ross.)

Seven

ENGAGEMENT IN THE GREATER DC COMMUNITY

While the Washington Canoe Club was established primarily to benefit its members and promote paddling, the club's history is also one of contributing to the Greater DC community. Early on, the club held theatricals, which contributed to the vibrant social life of early-20th-century Washington, and its regattas were major spectator events with no admission charge.

One particular club enterprise had enduring impact: a three-mile swimming race from the Chain Bridge to the Aqueduct Bridge. Initiated in 1911 by the WCC, the demanding and even dangerous race gained presidential sponsorship in 1925 and was sanctioned as the "national championship" contest. A second President's Cup race for powerboats debuted in 1926, and the two events, along with canoeing, rowing, and sailing competitions, were merged a few years later into the President's Cup Regatta, a major annual festival for the city that attracted national participation and large crowds for the next half-century.

Long-distance expeditions have on several occasions connected with the WCC as they journeyed to the nation's capital to promote a cause. One of the "Immortal Nine" on the historic 1954 hike to establish the C&O Canal park was a WCC member. More recently, weary but undaunted paddling and sailing crews have arrived at the WCC from as far away as Ottawa, northern Minnesota, and Honolulu. They have found a warm welcome at the WCC and used the club as the venue from which to publicize their causes.

WCC members have played an indispensable role in river safety over the years, complementing police and fire rescue teams as the first responders to on-river accidents and calamities. Many longtime members have personal stories of fishing fellow boaters out of the river after minor mishaps, and a number have actually saved lives. This is a tremendous service to the DC community.

In recent years, the club has expanded its mission of growing paddle sports by hosting youth groups, wounded warrior competitions, and river clean-ups.

While WCC paddlers have brought glory and renown to Washington through their racing prowess, the club also has a significant, though quieter, record of contributing to the general welfare of the city.

SPECTATOR SPORT. By the 1920s, canoe racing had become a major part of the sporting scene for DC residents, and there was no admission charge to watch the races. Here, well-dressed onlookers gather on land and water (at what appears to be Haines Point) for a regatta. The press gave extensive coverage as teams from East Coast cities and Canada traveled to compete with the WCC and other DC clubs. (Courtesy of Dan and Bonnie Havens.)

SERVING A THIRSTY CITY. The WCC had its own bootlegger named Bill Snow during the years of Prohibition (1920–1933) who, according to Frank Havens, "had a great booze-maker down the river on the Maryland side". Snow would pick up an order there and make the delivery to the WCC dock. Violation of the federal law was widespread but was not without its problems for the WCC; in 1926, the club worried that "some members are becoming intoxicated; in addition to the reputation the Club is receiving, there is always the danger of a raid by the police." (Courtesy of Dan and Bonnie Havens.)

CANOEING ON CANAL. Dressed up WCC "sailors" pose in front of one of the 74 lift locks of the C&O Canal, which sits just above the WCC boathouse. The canal, which was still used commercially by barges towed by mules until 1924, provided an alternative to paddling on the Potomac for early WCC members seeking a more tranquil experience or a place to train during times of high water or wind on the river. (Courtesy of the William "Dusty" Rhodes family.)

SAVING THE CANAL. In the early 1950s, there was a major push to convert the corridor of the abandoned C&O Canal to a four-lane scenic parkway. In 1954, WCCer Grant Conway (far left) was one of nine men (the "Immortal Nine") who hiked the entire 185-mile canal towpath to advocate for its protection; the historic trek's leader was Supreme Court justice William O. Douglas (fourth from right). The campaign succeeded, and the canal was designated a national historical park in 1971. (Courtesy of National Park Service, Chesapeake & Ohio National Historical Park.)

The First Annual

PRESIDENT'S RACE

A Three Mile Swim

from

Chain Bridge to Georgetown

In the Potomac River

Held by

THE WASHINGTON CANOE CLUB

Saturday August 22nd 1925

Sanctioned and Directed
by

THE AMATEUR ATHLETIC UNION
as
The National Long Distance Team Swimming Championship.

PRICE TWENTY-FIVE CENTS

NATIONAL CHAMPIONSHIP SWIM RACE. Always eager for opportunities to compete, the WCC in 1911 initiated a challenging three-mile swim race from the Chain Bridge to the Key Bridge. WCC swimmers won the first several races. As interest grew and teams came from as far away as New York, the WCC petitioned Pres. Calvin Coolidge in 1925 to sponsor the race, and he agreed, granting his "permission to place in competition the President's Cup as a trophy for the swimming competition on the Potomac River." Swimming's national governing body, the Amateur Athletic Union, designated the event as the national championship, and it is considered the first sanctioned long-distance swim race in the United States. A year later, a second President's Cup for speedboat racing was introduced, and in the 1930s, with canoeing, rowing, and sailing added to the program, the two events were merged as the President's Cup Regatta. The annual regatta drew large crowds for another 40 years. For safety reasons, the swim race was moved downstream in 1930 to flatter water in front of the WCC. Later, water quality concerns forced the race to be moved to a swimming pool venue. (Courtesy of the Charles Lundmark family.)

CHAIN BRIDGE SWIM START. Swimmers and their supporters prepare for the start of the President's Cup three-mile swim in the 1920s on a specially constructed platform. The steel truss bridge pictured was the seventh of eight bridges crossing the Potomac River at this site, dating back to 1797. Chains were used to suspend the roadway in earlier 19th-century spans, giving the bridge its name. A higher bridge replaced this one in 1939. (Courtesy of the William "Dusty" Rhodes family.)

TURBULENT WATERS. Racers (described in a contemporary account as "dare-devils") navigate the Potomac just below the Chain Bridge. The river here is unusually swift, with strong currents and undertows; the *Guinness Book of World Records* at one time recognized this section for its velocity. The swim race was usually held in August during the low-water period on the Potomac, making it somewhat safer. But in 1930, the event was moved to a triangular course downriver to reduce risk. (Courtesy of WCC.)

WCC, First Responder. Two unidentified WCC members hang on for dear life near Little Falls after an accident; one is holding the bow of their wrecked canoe. The WCC, with its location on a heavily boated section of the Potomac, has provided a critical community service in helping boaters in distress. With local rescue squads usually a phone call away, WCC members are often first on the scene. Many club members have stories of rendering assistance after simple canoe tip-overs or in life-threatening situations. (Courtesy of WCC.)

Primed to Rescue. WCC coach Matt West was at the club dock in June 1996 when he was alerted to an emergency; a local man had jumped from the Key Bridge in a suicide attempt and was in the water. West had recently completed a life-saving course and rushed to the scene in a club launch. He remembers that "on my way to him I saw him go under water several times; he was pretty close to going down and not coming back up." (Courtesy of Blaise Rhodes.)

A LIFE SAVED. With two collapsed lungs and broken ribs, Kyle Walton was seriously injured after his suicide jump. West lept into the water and pinned the badly bleeding Walton to the boat to keep him afloat until rescuers arrived (West, left, and Walton demonstrate the pinning position, above, at a recent reunion). Walton had to be evacuated by police and fire rescue teams. As he recovered (and was feeling very grateful to be alive), Walton wanted to know who his rescuer was, knowing only that the name was "Matt." They ultimately connected, and once Walton recovered, he nominated West for a Red Cross award (below) signed by Pres. Bill Clinton. West and Walton became lifelong friends; says Walton, "I got to live because Matt was there for me." (Both, courtesy of Mary Rollefson.)

A group of expert canoists steps ashore after testing a 24-foot war canoe similar to the craft in which nine servicemen died March 6.A board of inquiry viewed test.

4 More Bodies Found In River Near Quantico

WCC Safety Expertise. After a 1968 war canoe accident in which nine Marine paddlers drowned, the WCC was asked by a court of inquiry to help investigate. WCC volunteers provided a safety demonstration (at left) near the Marines' Quantico base on the Potomac, where the tragedy occurred. The WCCers showed that the craft was very seaworthy with a trained crew, even in waves, but that the inexperience of the Marines and the paralyzing shock of 36-degree water were probably the causes of the disaster. (Courtesy of *Washington Star* Collection, copyright *Washington Post*, reprinted with permission of DCPL.)

Safe Haven for Weary Paddlers. The WCC over the years has been the welcoming final port for long-distance paddling expeditions as they reach the nation's capital. In 2012, a group of Canadian environmentalists paddled a replica voyageur canoe over 1,100 miles from Ottawa to Washington to highlight water issues. Above, activists Dave and Amy Freeman arrived at the WCC on a cold, wet December day in 2014 after a 101-day paddle from northern Minnesota. They were publicizing a campaign to save Minnesota's million-acre Boundary Waters Canoe Wilderness Area from mining threats. (Courtesy of Northeast Minnesotans for Wilderness.)

HOKULEA FROM HAWAII, 2016. Sailing up the Potomac to its DC port of call, the WCC, is the *Hokulea*. A 61-foot-long, traditional Polynesian double-hulled sailing canoe, the *Hokulea* trains young Hawaiians and others in the ancient navigational arts that allowed Polynesians to colonize islands throughout the Pacific. The vessel's DC visit was a part of her 60,000-mile, four-year worldwide voyage. A fleet of WCC paddle craft escorted the *Hokulea* to the club. (Courtesy of Blaise Rhodes.)

EDUCATION AT WCC. WCCers, VIPs, and a local Hawaiian school, Halau O' Aulani, along with the Polynesian Voyaging Society, celebrated the *Hokulea*'s arrival with traditional blessings and through dance and music. Docked at the WCC for over a week, the *Hokulea* hosted almost 1,000 schoolchildren and other visitors who went aboard to learn about Hawaiian culture, the plight of the world's oceans, and long-distance sea travel on a small craft without modern conveniences. (Courtesy of Joe Cafferata.)

INTRODUCTION TO PADDLE SPORT. A group of summer campers from the Jubilee Housing Youth Services summer program in Adams Morgan prepares to launch and learn basic canoe paddling and safety skills at the canoe club. The canoeing program was preceded by a month of swimming lessons. Over the years, the WCC has joined with various nonprofit organizations to bring the challenges and excitement of paddling to youth who have no regular access to the river; a club program in the early 1970s brought inner-city youth to Bolling Air Force Base on the Anacostia River. For these Jubilee campers, the training session at the WCC is followed by an all-day outing on the Shenandoah River (below), where the kids enjoy swimming as well as negotiating mild whitewater. (Left, courtesy of the author; below, courtesy of Dickson Carroll.)

COMMUNITY FUNDRAISING. The WCC has been committed to giving back to the Greater DC community. One way has been to support and help host the Waterman's Paddle for Humanity during its 2011–2013 visits to DC. A touring SUP race with national and international competitors, the Waterman's Paddle raises money for local charities chosen by the host city director and for SurfAid International. The canoe club was the venue for the Waterman's Paddle's opening reception for two years. (Courtesy of Timmy Summers.)

CLEANING UP THE POTOMAC. Elite WCC paddlers Lisa Ramm (left) and Ann Armstrong (right) were among the WCC participants in a recent clean-up of the Potomac River organized by the Alice Ferguson Foundation. Each spring, club volunteers join hundreds of others up and down the Potomac and its tributaries to pick up trash in and along the river. The WCC is a temporary repository for the accumulated trash. (Courtesy of Blaise Rhodes.)

WOUNDED AND DISABLED VETERANS. Each year, the WCC hosts Team River Runner, a nonprofit dedicated to providing all veterans and their families an opportunity to find health, healing, community purpose, and new challenges. The group, assisted by WCC volunteers, organizes a biathlon for disabled veterans at the WCC, which includes a kayak and stand-up paddle race and a run or hand crank segment on the Capital Crescent Trail. Adaptive paddle sports, including paddling in modified kayaks, allow the veterans to get the benefits of being on the water and competing. (Above, courtesy of Blaise Rhodes; below, courtesy of Team River Runner.)

Eight

THE SPIRIT TO ENDURE

Among the apt descriptions for the Washington Canoe Club is "survivor," for both the boathouse and the social entity. From its beginning, the boathouse has been buffeted by hurricanes, ice jams, and floods and had one close call with a fire. On top of that, a growing metropolis has again and again posed existential threats to the building, and political and social winds have buffeted the club.

The Three Sisters Bridge, proposed in the 1960s, would have run a major highway approach right through WCC's home but was dropped after fierce opposition. Another riverside infrastructure project—the massive Dulles Interceptor Sewer—had to be rerouted to avoid the building. Water quality concerns in the mid-20th century threatened to make the Potomac too polluted for human contact. Abandonment of the Georgetown Spur railroad right-of-way in the 1980s made shoreline and road development near the club a distinct possibility. Various construction and repair projects adjacent to the WCC have created on-again, off-again disruptions.

Parallel with these challenges have been changes in land values and public opinion. What was at one time a backwater location along a railroad spur has become prime real estate on the Georgetown waterfront. At the same time, public attitudes about preservation of green space and the need for public access to the river have evolved. Occupancy of public land (within a national park unit) by a private entity became a flash point in the early 21st century, and the very survival of the WCC on its current site was at stake.

The story is not over. The DC Water and Sewer Authority plans to build a deep tunnel under the Georgetown waterfront with the access shaft squarely in the WCC driveway. And after several years of negotiation, the club signed a 60-year lease with the National Park Service in 2019 to remain in its historic location. It was a big step forward, but now begins the enormous challenge of financing the restoration of its deteriorated boathouse.

Other Georgetown boathouses have succumbed to flood, fire, ice, decay, and development pressures, but the WCC has endured. The club is now vital and thriving. A membership committed to the club's strong volunteer ethic, to its competitive and social traditions, and now embracing its role as keeper of the historic boathouse seems well positioned to ensure a bright future for the Washington Canoe Club.

NATURAL DISASTERS. The historic Potomac ice jam of 1918 folded the shed roof (above, center) and crushed the main structure of Dempsey's Boathouse but mostly spared the WCC. Spectators witnessed the devastation from the safety of the Aqueduct Bridge. Another ice floe in 1957 pushed the WCC boathouse off its piers; members used jacks borrowed from the railroad to reset it in its original location. The historic Hurricane Agnes flood of 1972 (below) inundated the WCC boathouse, even as some brave souls watched from the balcony. The club's boathouse has had many narrow escapes from floods and ice in its century-plus history, events that have done in dozens of other riverside shacks, docks, and boathouses. High waters may well increase in the future, with the warming planet bringing rising sea levels and changing weather patterns. (Above, courtesy of Library of Congress, below, courtesy of Catherine Newdorp Brosius.)

HIGHWAY PLANS. The 1960s brought a new threat to the WCC: a proposed interstate highway crossing the Potomac just half a mile upriver of the club, with access ramps running through the boathouse. Controversy over the planned Three Sisters Bridge (artist rendering above, looking toward the DC shore) went on for a decade. The WCC joined riverside protests led by the Canoe Cruisers Association and other groups, and the bridge plan was eventually dropped. (Courtesy of DC Department of Transportation.)

FIRE. Fire has been an ever-present concern for old buildings in DC, including the WCC; its all-wood structure and the difficulty of fire equipment reaching it quickly make the boathouse particularly vulnerable. Other DC-area boathouses—the High Island Canoe Club, near Little Falls; Old Dominion Boat Club in Alexandria; and Dempsey's in Georgetown (burning above)—all suffered catastrophic fires at least once. (Courtesy of *Washington Evening Star* Collection, copyright *Washington Post*, reprinted with permission of DCPL.)

END OF THE RAILROAD ERA. A freight train rolls along the Georgetown Spur past Dempsey's Boathouse and the WCC (background) in 1947. The rail line played a significant part in the WCC's history for 100 years. Early on, club members walked along or crossed the tracks to reach the boathouse, and possibly supplies were delivered and canoes transported on the spur. The last train ran in 1985, and the line was abandoned. Converted to the now-popular Capital Crescent Trail (below) around 1990, this rail-trail gives WCC members a new bicycle or pedestrian option to reach the club, connecting them to a vast regional trail system. The trail provides a place to cross-train and a ready-made venue for biathlon events but has also introduced heavy use to what had once been the out-of-the-way environs of the club. (Above, courtesy of Randolph Routt, *Washington Evening Star* photographer; below, courtesy of Mary Rollefson.)

INFRASTRUCTURE. In the late 1960s, the local sewer authority installed a massive, eight-foot-diameter sewer line along the Potomac shore to carry waste from the new Dulles Airport to a treatment facility in DC. The WCC's boathouse was directly in the path but again dodged a bullet; the Dulles Connector alignment was revised to avoid the landmark structure. Ironically, the project benefited the WCC, as the concrete pad poured to cover the pipe created an expansive riverside space for the club. (Courtesy of DC Water and Sewer Authority.)

DETERIORATION. The bracing in the WCC ballroom, installed by the National Park Service (NPS) in 2011–2102, attests to the declining condition of the boathouse, which as of 2019 had been unoccupied for 10 years. The club finally concluded a 60-year lease with the NPS in 2019, so it can now begin its major project: restoring the boathouse to its former glory. (Courtesy of Historic American Building Survey, National Park Service.)

CHANGED WATERFRONT VALUES. In this 1923 view looking east from the Key Bridge, Georgetown was still the commercial and industrial zone it had been for more than two centuries, and the WCC (not pictured) occupied a quiet corner at its upper end. As late as 1950, the assessed value of the WCC boathouse was only $875. With the establishment of the C&O Canal park in 1971 and the transformation of the Georgetown waterfront in the late 20th century (below) to a park and high-end commercial development, the WCC's out-of-the-way refuge on the edge became prized real estate, bringing unwanted attention to the club. In addition, the National Park Service came under pressure to eliminate the use of public land by a private entity like the WCC. The WCC's status as a century-old institution, with a strong Olympic tradition and occupying a landmark boathouse, allowed it to survive through some challenging times. (Above, courtesy of Library of Congress; below, courtesy of Mary Rollefson.)

SPIRIT TO ENDURE. WCC paddlers Jay Gopal (front) and Doug Brooks (back) endure the grind of the 70-mile General Clinton marathon race in 2018. The club, too, must endure challenges. The pen-and-ink drawing below by Robert J. Carr conveys a deceptively serene scene, for life on the Potomac waterfront is likely to always bring new hurdles for the WCC. Never fully secure, the club will need vigilance and resilience. But with its fully engaged, energetic, and loyal membership, its robust competitive and youth programs, and a long tradition of facing and overcoming daunting challenges, the WCC seems more than ready to prosper for another century or more. (Above, courtesy of Blaise Rhodes; below, courtesy of WCC.)

The Washington Canoe Club

Discover Thousands of Local History Books Featuring Millions of Vintage Images

Arcadia Publishing, the leading local history publisher in the United States, is committed to making history accessible and meaningful through publishing books that celebrate and preserve the heritage of America's people and places.

Find more books like this at
www.arcadiapublishing.com

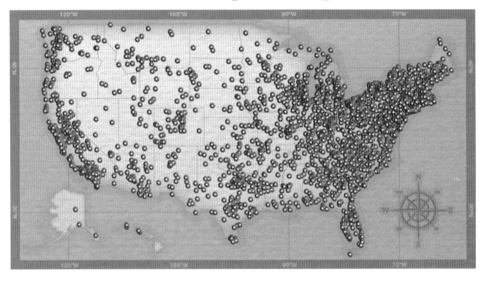

Search for your hometown history, your old stomping grounds, and even your favorite sports team.